High Jumps and Dumbbells

High Jumps and Dumbbells

by Joan Simons

with illustrations by Joyce L. Bond

1979
Alpine Publications
1901 South Garfield
Loveland, Colorado 80537

The characters and incidents in this book are fictional and entirely the product of the author's imagination. They have no relation to any person or event in real life, except for the character of Sissy, who is very real indeed.

Chapters 1 through 11 were published in serial form in *The Sheltie Special,* Tentagel Publications, Inc., Menlo Park, California, under the titles "Sissie of High Point" and "Sissie: Obedience Dog," during 1976 and 1977.

International Standard Book Number 0-931866-04-9
Library of Congress Catalog Card Number 79-55024

Copyright ©1979 by Alpine Publications, 1901 South Garfield, Loveland, CO. All rights reserved. No part of this book may be reproduced in any manner whatsoever without written permission from the publisher, except in the case of brief quotations embodied in critical articles and reviews.

First edition 1979.
Printed in the United States of America.

*For my mother,
who finally learned to like dog shows*

Contents

	Preface... ix
1	The Beginning... 1
2	A Matter of Survival.................................... 6
3	The Newcomers.. 11
4	The Trespassers... 16
5	The Winner.. 23
6	To Catch A Thief.. 28
7	A Trick or Two.. 34
8	A Day in Court.. 41
9	The Wonder Dog... 48
10	A Well-Trained Dog..................................... 57
11	Gentleman Jim, the Saint, and the Double Zinger.. 63
12	A Matter of Relevance................................. 70
13	The Ice Princess.. 77
14	A Boy and His Dog..................................... 85
15	The Good Sport... 94
16	Of Tough Judges, Fashion, and the Green-eyed Monster.................................. 99
17	The Dark Hours... 106
18	No Place to Go But Up................................. 111
19	The Test... 115

20	The Cow Jumped Over the Moon	120
21	An Interpretation of Rules	126
22	The Old Order Changeth	133
	About The Author	139

Preface

*H*igh Jumps and Dumbbells is the story of a Sheltie; in fact, it is the story of a particular Sheltie. But it is also about the sport of dog obedience, training one's dog not only to obey basic commands such as "Heel" and "stay" but to become part of a smoothly working dog-handler team in obedience competition. Showing a dog to a Championship title in conformation is thrilling; striving for the obedience titles of Companion Dog, Companion Dog Excellent, Utility Dog, Tracking Dog, and the coveted Obedience Trial Championship—all are equally challenging and enticing goals. And obedience showing yields a wonderful plus: the close relationship that grows between handler and dog.

Sissie's story is my "thank you" to the sport of dog obedience and to all of my friends in the world of dogs. Through Paul and Irma Boax of the Allegheny County All-Breed Training Club I was initiated into obedience training with my first Sheltie, Laddie. Through Marie Miller and the late A. Raymond Miller of Pixie Dell, I entered the exciting world of conformation showing with two lovely Shelties: first Lotus, Sissie's mother, and later Dolly, who still wakes me each day with her cold muzzle and soft whining for a biscuit.

Several dog trainers also have earned my gratitude. Thank you to Rosalind Cich of Tall Oaks for her sensitive direction of Sissie's training; to Wayne Chandler and Thelma Luck of the Greater Milwaukee Shetland Sheepdog Club; and to Jack Love, Art Chanos, Robert Streeter, and the late Tony Stahl — dedicated, hard-working trainers of the K-9 Obedience Training Club of Menomonee Falls. Thank you, too, Emma Brodzeller, for your special help and encouragement. And thank you Betty McKinney and Barbara Rieseberg of Alpine Publications, for your faith in Sissie's story.

In obedience, the relationship between handler and dog is very special. It is always a good time for Sissie and me when the collar, leash, and dumbbell are produced from the hall closet, signaling a lesson. Sissie leaps up, yelping her excitement. I shush her. She snakes her slender muzzle through the collar, eager to begin. Finally the collar is in place, the lead snapped on.

"Sissie, heel!" I stride out left foot first.

Sissie swings to heel, and we move out together — as a team.

JOAN SIMONS
Wauwatosa, Wisconsin

1

The Beginning

Sissie wriggled into the world eagerly, a sable and white Sheltie pup ready for adventure. Even in the kind hands of Jan Dalton and her husband Gil, two English teachers who raised Shetland sheepdogs as a hobby, Sissie squirmed and squealed — a sticky, wet, newborn pup, frightened and blind. Jan dried the little female pup with a soft towel, then placed her on a heating pad to protect her from the early spring chill.

It was a small litter, only four pups, which meant that each pup would have plenty of milk and attention. Sissie's mother, a beautiful black, white, and tan Sheltie named Lotus, began licking the puppies and taking care of them immediately.

While Lotus looked on anxiously, Gil picked up each puppy, wondering what to name each one.

"A dog's name should reflect his personality or appearance," he said.

Jan agreed, and the two of them tried to think of good names. The biggest puppy they called Lancer. The smallest male became Teddy. The middle-sized scrappy fellow already groping for a way out of his box was, they agreed, the Pilot of the litter. All three males were black, white, and tan like their mother.

Then Gil picked up the wriggling brown and white female.

"With three black and white brothers, she seems to be the fair sister," Jan observed.

"That's it," Gil said.

"What's what?" puzzled Jan, smiling at the noisy, mewing puppy.

"Little Sister," Gil answered.

"How about Sissie for short?" Jan suggested.

"I've got it — we'll name her Sissie of High Point."

1

"What's High Point?"

"High Point will be the name of our kennel some day. This is our first High Point litter." His eyes looked dreamy as he thought about the Sheltie kennel that he and Jan hoped to found.

Jan nodded agreement. The puppies were named.

At first Sissie's world was small. The furry warmth of her mother and milk when she was hungry were all that she needed. Sometimes in scrambling for milk, Lancer and Pilot shoved her rudely so that she rolled squealing to the corner of the box. Then, blind, she had to crawl back to the center of her world. She loved the roughness of her mother's tongue licking her again and again, keeping her clean and warm.

When Sissie was eight days old, she could see the three rude brothers that had been pushing her around so fiercely. She learned how to weasel under them to get to her mother's side, and once she was sucking milk, there was no budging her. And so she thrived.

Gradually, Sissie became aware of Gil's kind, low voice and Jan's soothing, higher voice cooing over the puppies. Now that Lotus left her alone more and more, Sissie would desperately try to climb the slippery side of the cardboard box to look for her mother. Once she managed to get her forepaws over the edge, but then she just hung on until she tumbled back onto Lancer, who didn't appreciate having his nap interrupted. The nip that he gave Sissie wasn't playful.

But Lotus always returned to her puppies, and Sissie found comfort once more snuggled against her beautiful mother. Sissie loved her mother very much.

Soon it was warm enough for the puppies to play outside in the welcome Wisconsin spring. Sissie loved the warmth of the sun, even though her world suddenly had become frighteningly large.

As the puppies tumbled through the grass, dodging the lawn chairs and jumping over twigs from the giant willow tree, Lotus taught them survival tactics: how to lunge for the throat of an attacker and how to grab an enemy's leg and throw him off balance. Lotus would bump into the puppies, knock them down, then offer her throat to their weak, fumbling jaws.

They loved this new game and began playing it with each other. Sissie would bowl over Teddy, and then Lancer, the strongest, would send them both snout over heels. Lotus would stand by, looking pleased that her puppies were learning so quickly.

One day a lady came to see the puppies and picked up Pilot and hugged him, talking to him in the high, cooing voice that Jan sometimes used. Jan and Gil looked sad when they said good-by to Pilot, but they couldn't keep all of the puppies. Soon afterwards, the same thing happened to Teddy, only it was a little boy who hugged Sissie's brother happily.

Only Sissie and Lancer were left. They had a wonderful summer playing with each other and with Cindy and Michael from next door. When four-year-old Michael would throw the puppies' favorite toy — one of Gil's old socks knotted in the middle — Sissie would race Lancer to the sock. Even though Lancer always won the race, Sissie learned to grab the loose end of the sock and hold on like a bulldog in a running tug-of-war with Lancer all the way back to Michael. Michael would laugh and throw the sock again.

The puppies grew fast. Soon both were leggy and awkward and were beginning to lose their fluffy puppy coats and grow glossy permanent ones. Their stubby puppy heads lengthened to graceful, collie-like heads. Gil and Jan thought that Lancer was turning into a fine show dog, but Sissie was not quite the same story.

For Sissie seemed to be all legs, and she was very clumsy. She couldn't catch the knotted sock in midair the way that Lotus or Lancer could. Lotus could leap up to catch the sock at just the right time, but when Gil threw the sock for Sissie, the ungainly puppy would leap into the air too soon, missing it completely. When she heard Gil and Jan laughing at her, she slunk to Gil, her ears back dejectedly and her eyes begging forgiveness. Gil would pick her up and pet her until she felt better.

One early fall day a man and woman came with their little girl to see the puppies. It was Lancer that the child fell in love with. When Sissie saw her pick up Lancer, cuddle him, and rub her chin against his soft ears, she retreated to Gil, straddling his left foot. She sensed that Lancer would be taken away, and she was right.

After Lancer had gone, Sissie was very lonesome. She loped from room to room, sniffing under beds and behind couches where Lancer had played. That night Sissie snuggled extra close to her mother.

Now, however, Sissie received twice as much attention from everyone. Lotus, of course, as "dog-in-chief" of the household, was still the only one allowed on the red leather couch in the den. And Lotus was always given first turn at catching the old knotted sock. Every morning Gil and Jan petted Lotus first, while Sissie impatiently waited her turn.

In September, when Sissie was four months old, she noticed a change in Lotus's attitude toward her. Up to now, when they had eaten dinner side by side, Sissie had freely stolen choice food from her mother's dish. But one day when Sissie was about to snatch a morsel of liver from Lotus's bowl, she heard a low growl. She froze. Lotus's fangs were bared, her lip curled above the fangs, wrinkled and quivering; her head hung low, with the hackles on the back of her neck bristling. Lotus menaced Sissie as she would any stranger who threatened to steal her food.

Sissie backed off, stunned to realize that she was no longer her mother's pampered baby.

That evening while Gil and Jan were eating dinner, Sissie stretched out across Gil's foot. Henceforth this would be her favorite resting place.

Autumn swept in brisk and cool, providing crunchy mounds of leaves for Sissie to leap into, roll in, and scatter; that is, until Gil, waving his rake, chased her away.

Sissie was very leggy now and more awkward than ever. Shelties are supposed to look like miniature collies, but no one ever said of Sissie, "Look at the little collie," as they said of Lotus. People were more likely to ask, "What kind of dog is that?" Sissie, completely unsure of herself, was ashamed to stand beside her beautiful, graceful mother.

In spite of Sissie's awkwardness, however, the Daltons decided to keep her as a pet; that is, if the growing scrappiness between Lotus and Sissie didn't erupt into war.

Sissie was such a happy puppy most of the time that at first she scarcely minded Lotus's growing hostility. As fall marched toward winter, however, Sissie thought that Lotus was getting downright nasty. The older dog would chase Sissie out of the den, nipping and growling at the confused puppy. Sissie let her alone when she was in such a mood and instead followed Jan. Jan would talk to Sissie and pause frequently to rumple Sissie's silken ears, which always made the gangling puppy feel better.

Sissie was six months old now — very nearly grown up.

2

A Matter of Survival

It was not easy for a dog whose ancestors herded sheep in the rugged hills of Scotland and the Shetland Islands, sharing their masters' outdoor lives, to enjoy life in a modern suburb or city where dogs must be constantly leashed and confined. Although Sissie had a large yard the fence around it depressed her.

As cool October air swept away the musky heat of the Wisconsin Indian summer, Sissie felt restless. Molelike, she dug a hole under the fence. Little by little the hole grew, concealed by weeds. The day that Sissie started to squeeze through, however, Jan saw her from the kitchen window. And that was the end of *that* little adventure.

Rainy days, when there seemed to be nothing for an active young dog to do indoors, were especially miserable. Therefore, when Sissie discovered The Place, her desire to get out was uncontrollable.

* * * *

Jan and Gil were looking for a new home with more land where they could establish their kennel, but in the meantime there was no place nearby to take two frisky Shelties for a daily romp.

One night they sat down with pen, paper, and bankbook and tried to figure out a way to buy a home far enough out in the suburbs beyond zoning restrictions.

"Jan, it just doesn't add up yet," Gil moaned, filling sheet after sheet with figures.

"Even with both of us teaching? And putting off having a family for a few years?"

"The down payment would wipe us out. If we owned this home it would be our down payment. As it is, all we've got to show for living here is a pile of rent receipts."

"OK, we'll just keep saving. And be prepared to eat beans and noodles more often, instead of meat."

While they worked and saved, they had to make the best of their present location. Every evening after supper Gil would drive Sissie and Lotus to a wooded area about three miles away where the dogs could run and explore. The Place, owned by the nearby stone quarry, was no longer used because the daily blastings of limestone in the quarry made the area unfit for homes. For city dogs, The Place was a paradise where they could experience the wild ways of nature, if only for a little while.

Sissie loved The Place. She loved to root under piles of amber leaves or try to chew the hard shells of acorns. Giant, twisted roots bore the scent of wild animals. Not accustomed to hunting but nevertheless sharp-nosed, the Shelties did not know what to do when a squirrel or rabbit darted for cover. Sissie barked a lot and chased the swift little creatures to no avail.

But the flu became the enemy of these wonderful outings.

One day Gil came home feeling very tired and postponed that evening's walk. After dinner, Sissie ran to the door, whining and eager for her usual ramble in the woods.

"No, Sissie, not tonight," groaned Gil, who was feeling terrible. He lay on the den couch covered with warm blankets, alternately shivering and sweating.

Sissie hopefully nuzzled his leg.

"Go away, Sissie," he objected. Sissie tried licking his fingers to coax him to take her for her walk.

"No, Sissie, don't bother me," snapped Gil.

Sissie slumped to the floor, disappointed. She comforted herself by taking a nap beside the couch where her sick master lay.

Gil was sick all week, and Sissie had no rambles at The Place. She became desperate, and Saturday morning she found her opportunity for escape.

Jan was airing blankets and winter coats to get them ready for winter use. While she was hanging blankets on the line, the cleaner drove into the driveway to deliver Gil's slacks and jacket. Jan went into the house to get some money.

Although Lotus and Sissie barked dutifully, they knew the deliveryman and wagged their tails. Sissie ran to the gate, and *it was unlatched.* With just the slightest push Sissie was out. Since no one was paying any attention to her, there seemed no reason why she shouldn't visit The Place by herself. Lotus hung back, unwilling to break the rules, so Sissie began her trek alone.

As if instinctively, she knew which direction to take. Moving in and out of side streets, dodging cars, disregarding "keep off the grass" signs, she moved closer and closer to her goal. In less than an hour she arrived at The Place, and loping first to the creek that harbored The Place's frog and tadpole population, she drank her fill of clear, pure water and lay down to rest.

She could hardly believe her good luck. Once rested, she explored mysterious new parts of The Place, occasionally startling a chipmunk or rabbit. She was having a wonderful time.

The sudden leap of a rabbit from a clump of weeds that she was sniffing toppled Sissie off balance. As she twisted to right herself, she tumbled against a bush. Prickly fingers seized her and held her motionless. Panic-stricken, Sissie lunged. The excruciating pain of spiked burrs ripping into the soft flesh of her belly and pulling the soft hairs hurled her onto the ground whimpering.

Instinct governed her now, and she kept quiet lest, trapped in this way, she become easy prey for enemies. Every effort to escape the burr nest brought pain. With every motion new burrs grasped her fine hair until she was a complete prisoner.

Hours passed. Suddenly, a tremendous roar blasted the air, shaking the trapped puppy into a frenzy of terror. While explosions from the nearby quarry ripped the earth, Sissie clung to the quivering ground beneath her, her eyes wild with fright, her tongue lolling out the side of her mouth.

Then the heavings of the earth stopped and quiet returned. Sissie tried again to escape from her trap.

This time she had a plan. She began to chew through each burr-tangled strand of hair, starting with her forelegs and working back toward her belly. As she gnawed the tight hairs close to the burr itself, she whimpered with pain.

Carefully, Sissie grasped each hateful burr between her front teeth, lifted it out of its bed of matted hair, and spat it out as far as possible. Slowly but steadily she worked until both forelegs were freed. Finally, she could sit up and gnaw on the burrs that clutched her tail.

From chewing off so much of her own hair, her tongue had become matted with hair and her throat was parched. She knew that she *must* free herself.

In the darkness, cicadas roared, the bullfrogs belched, but Sissie worked with a dedication that deafened her to all distractions. *She was almost free.* Gathering all four legs beneath her, she struggled upward on stiff, cramped muscles, lurched forward, and leaped clear. She was weak, trembling, and sore, but she was free.

For a while Sissie lay down to rest in a pile of cool rotting leaves, licking her red, blood-streaked belly. A few burrs still clung tenaciously to her tail, but there were more important matters to attend to now. Sissie had to get home.

Wearily, the little Sheltie rose to her feet and, stiff and sore, started for home. She followed quite closely the route that she had taken that morning, leaving the road several times to rest on a cool lawn. It was very late — no one walked the streets; traffic was sparse; and scarecely a light shone from the dim, silent houses.

The approach of a moving light sent Sissie burrowing deep into a pile of leaves, ready to flee or fight if this new enemy should come too close. She prepared to battle for survival and a chance to get home again. The faint padding became louder, until with a rush the strange dog was on Sissie, bowling her over. Sissie whimpered with joy. It was Lotus, who had caught Sissie's scent and tracked down the runaway, with Jan close behind. Sissie's ordeal was over.

3

The Newcomers

The down payment wiped out their savings, and the mortgage debt claimed a large chunk of their future earnings, but early in November Gil and Jan bought an old house far enough out of Milwaukee to give them two full acres — enough for the long-dreamed-of High Point Kennels.

On moving day, the young couple romped with the Shelties like preschoolers for the sheer joy of stretching out on their own, if mortgaged, grounds. Lotus and Sissie joined happily in the fun.

But within a few weeks the Daltons were discussing which of the two dogs had to go. The trouble did not surface immediately. In fact, after the confusion of moving was over, both dogs were busy and happy exploring their new home. Running busily from room to room, tracking down the ghosts of cats and sticky-fingered children, Sissie and Lotus forgot that they were frequently at odds with one another.

Outdoors, their excitement was even greater. The grounds sloped nearly an acre behind the house to a thick hedge of pussy willow and lilac, nearly bare now in the grayish light of November. Dead leaves held scents of birds and wild rabbits, promising marvelous summers to come. Sissie's full white ruff sparkled through the black leaves like a chalk mark, signaling to Jan where the dogs were playing.

But as the novelty of their new home wore off, Lotus became increasingly grouchy with Sissie. Jan and Gil were deeply troubled that their two loved pets weren't getting along with each other.

The next two months were the unhappiest of Sissie's short life. Lotus refused to have anything to do with her and became downright hostile. In a jealous rage one morning, the older dog chased Sissie out from under Gil's bed, then refused to let Sissie get near her bowl at dinner time. And worst of all for Sissie, Lotus refused to play with her.

During this difficult period, however, Sissie's coat began to grow, and Gil and Jan were pleased with her improved appearance.

"You know, Jan," Gil said one evening, "Sissie just might turn out to be a real beauty after all, — maybe even a Champion."

He leaned down and rumpled Sissie's ears. And then she was happy.

But although Sissie was beginning to look mature, she didn't always act mature. One gloomy Saturday afternoon, Jan locked Lotus and Sissie in the den while she went grocery shopping. Sissie took a nap, but when she awoke she was bored. As usual, Lotus refused to play.

Sissie knew that she mustn't chew the legs of the den couch or any of the furniture — a folded newspaper had taught her that lesson when she was a small puppy. That left only the large cardboard box bound with heavy cord standing in the corner. Sissie couldn't remember ever having been punished in connection with a cardboard box. It was certainly fair game.

When Jan returned home two hours later and opened the den door, her scream drove Sissie under the red leather couch for refuge. Lotus scooted out of the room as if pleading her innocence.

The cardboard box sagged in the corner, one side well chewed. But the object that brought horror to Jan's face was something identifiable only as a tooth-marked, brownish stick. Puzzled at first, Jan suddenly recognized the object as the "sword" of Gil's treasured swordfish that he had caught off the Florida coast last year.

Sissie was in disgrace.

Gil banished both dogs from the den and said that if Sissie damaged any more property, she would be sold. Puppyhood no longer excused her.

Sissie was miserable. Even the weather reflected her despair as black clouds signaled early snow squalls. The small migrating birds had gone; only the hungry hawks took to the air in squadrons along the coast of Lake Michigan as they headed south, seeking food.

Although Sissie still enjoyed playing outside, her banishment from the den plagued her. By the end of the week she was not the happy Sheltie that she had always been. Her tail hung limp. Although Gil pitied her, he would not relent.

"The sooner we find another home for Sissie, the better," he decreed. Still, he didn't advertise Sissie for sale.

The following Sunday, while Gil read the paper, Sissie moped outside the den door until Jan, feeling sorry for her, put the dogs outside. Lotus sniffed Sissie disdainfully and strolled away, leaving Sissie once more without a playmate. The sky was ominously purple, and the air was still. Only a faint line of laggard hawks lent movement to Sissie's world.

It would have been difficult to say whether Sissie first *saw* the rangy brown rabbit skimming the earth, or *heard* the flapping above her, or *felt* the rush of air as the great body swooped down through the yellowish light, but instantly Sissie knew as the great bird dived for the rabbit and missed, that her home was under attack. Barking loudly, both dogs sprang to defend their home against the menacing newcomer circling above them.

The hungry bird, cheated out of its rabbit, screamed in fury, then turned its attention to the new prey that flashed below, not even running away. The two dogs with their bright white markings were a prime target.

The great bird's wings covered the sky above Sissie. Lotus, judging the foe as too formidable even for a courageous Sheltie, retreated to the house. But Sissie spun to face the bird that now dived toward her, its great curved talons spread to seize its prey.

Still barking and growling fiercely, Sissie realized that she was no match for this dive-bombing fury. She ran for her life toward the house, her white legs and collar flashing through the dark leaves to make her an excellent target. Above her, the wing shadow widened as the bird prepared once again to strike.

The prey that he faced this time was a greater challenge than he had anticipated, however, for Jan, investigating the commotion, grabbed the mop that was drying against the back of the house and shook it at the bird, screaming "Shoo! Shoo!" hysterically.

The bird's talons seized the mop handle. Jan let go of the mop and screamed just as Gil reached her, taking aim with his rifle. The bird dropped the mop and wheeled in to attack.

Sissie crouched, waiting. As the incensed bird's wings whizzed past, Sissie leaped high into the air, clamped her jaws on something, heard the sudden deafening noise, felt a ripping between her teeth, then fell dizzily to earth at Gil's feet, belly up and completely winded.

Gil still held the smoking rifle aimed at the bird, which was disappearing in the distance. So swift and incredible had the incident been that Gil and Jan just stood there stunned.

Finally, Gil lowered his gun and went inside to call the humane society. Jan took the dogs into the house. Neighbors who had heard the gunshot called. Gil told them what had happened and warned them to keep their children and pets inside. All he knew was that the bird was too large to be a hawk.

Later that day, a team of men from the humane society cornered the warlike newcomer in a park, subdued it with a tranquilizer dart, and took the submitting eagle to the county zoo. Incredibly, the bird that had almost killed Sissie was a golden eagle with a wingspread of six feet — far off its course hunting for food. Eventually, the eagle would be released in a more natural setting.

Only after all the excitement was over did Gil realize what Sissie had brought into the house with her after the attack — a clutch of pinion feathers from the bird's wing tip, ragged but intact.

"It looks as though we have a new trophy," Gil proclaimed as he picked up the feathers and examined them. And later, when Gil and Jan talked over the event, they left the den door open. Sissie and Lotus hesitated. Sissie entered first and was not scolded.

Then Lotus curled up underneath the old mahogany desk, while Sissie sprawled in front of the couch for a much needed rest. The den was open territory to the dogs again.

A few evenings later Gil hung the eagle feathers — framed under glass on a white mat — above the den couch. Beside this new trophy he hung the tooth-marked swordfish. Jan smiled at the weird display.

"A man and his dog like to have their trophies where they can be admired," Gil explained, sensing her amusement.

"Oh," Jan answered with a smile.

The excitement of the eagle incident made them forget that only a few days ago they had been planning to find a new home for Sissie. And in their joy at being admitted to the den once more, Sissie and Lotus apparently forgot their differences. A crisis had been averted, at least temporarily. Contented, sprawled across Gil's left foot, Sissie let her eyes close drowsily.

4

The Trespassers

Immediately after Thanksgiving, Gil and Jan made formal application to the American Kennel Club for use of the kennel name "High Point". Since the name would have to be cleared for originality, among other requirements, they settled down to wait out a long period of red tape and suspense.

Their nerves were not soothed by the unusually severe winter. Sissie and Lotus loved snow, however, and when Jan returned home each day from her teaching job, the two Shelties burrowed in the snow until they popped up white as Samoyeds, then shook themselves back to sable and black again. As they played, their frost-covered whiskers glistened like needle-thin icicles.

Not until spring, when the snowdrifts melted, did Sissie and Lotus become acquainted with their new neighbors. And that was when the trouble started over the vacant lot behind their home.

Mr. Neville, who owned the lot, had made it clear that he wouldn't permit dogs on his land because he wanted it kept safe for wildlife. The Daltons readily agreed. The thicket was a refuge for pheasant, squirrels, and other small animals and birds. There were few paths. It was a beautiful paradise. The problem was that small children were drawn to the woods as if by a magnet.

Every Sunday afternoon, Mr. Neville's grandchildren, Ralph and Ann Marie, visited their grandparents. Ralph, eight years old, was the leader since Ann Marie was only four and one-half. Sneaking off to the woods soon became the children's favorite game.

When Gil and Jan moved into their new home, a great attraction was added to the children's visits to their grandparents — two lively Shelties to pet and play with. Ann Marie especially liked

Sissie, and Sissie loved the dainty, blond child who played with her each Sunday.

One glorious May Sunday, Jan, watching out of the kitchen window, saw Ann Marie enter the backyard to play with Sissie. Sissie eagerly ran to meet her playmate, the old sock dangling from the Sheltie's jaws. Jan meant to supervise the game, but she had English themes to correct. By the time she got around to looking outside again, Ann Marie was gone, and Lotus and Sissie stretched panting on the emerald lawn.

Suddenly, the dogs began barking, and Jan heard a faint wail that grew louder and clearer until there was no mistaking the terrified scream of a child in pain. She saw nothing from the kitchen window. Then she ran to the front door to see if the cries were coming from that direction. There stood Mr. Neville, carrying little Ann Marie. Her right leg dripped blood, and her face was red and twisted from crying. Mr. Neville rushed in with the child. Gil came running.

"I found her in your front yard," Mr. Neville gasped, almost too overcome with anger and exertion to continue.

"Look!" He pointed at Ann Marie's poor bloody leg. "This is what your beast has done to my grandchild!"

Mr. Neville's shoulders shook with shock and outrage. Gil took the child from him and laid her on the couch. Then he called his doctor, who lived only a few miles away and agreed to come immediately.

While waiting for the doctor, Gil washed the wound, definitely an animal bite.

"Our dogs didn't do this, Mr. Neville," Gil tried to calm the old man. "Another dog or perhaps a wild animal must have bitten Ann Marie."

Just then Sissie and Lotus ran into the living room to investigate. When Sissie tried sympathetically to lick Ann Marie's injured leg, the child, whose crying had almost stopped, began to scream anew.

"Doggie," she lisped between terrified shrieks, "Doggie *bit* me, doggie *hurt* Ann Marie. Doggie go away!"

And she continued screaming until Sissie, cringing with fright and surprise, was led, ears flat against her head, tail between her legs, out of the room.

The Daltons didn't know what to say. Surely Sissie couldn't have hurt this child. But Ann Marie herself had identified her attacker. What had happened? Was the mistake their own in allowing the dogs too much freedom?

The doctor treated the wound, which was not deep. However, there was danger of infection and, though they hesitated to say the word, the lurking danger of rabies.

"Has Sissie been inoculated for rabies?" Mr. Neville asked.

"No," Gil admitted. "But I know that my dogs haven't been in contact with rabid animals."

"The chances are," said the doctor, applying a light dressing to the wound, "that Ann Marie was bitten by a wild animal. But since it's unlikely that this animal will be found, we should take every precaution."

"Why can't we just observe Sissie to see if she develops symptoms?" asked Mr. Neville sourly. "Isn't that the way dog bites are usually handled?"

"That's the usual way, Mr. Neville," the doctor agreed, "but if there's any doubt about what animal bit the child, then we must assume the possibility of real danger."

"Could the woods be searched?" Gil suggested. He was certain that Sissie was innocent, but if she wasn't cleared of the charges against her, Mr. Neville could seek court action to have her destroyed.

"Don't be foolish," shouted Mr. Neville, his face lined with worry. "Ann Marie said that the *doggie* bit her, and she pointed at that brown and white miniature collie of yours. Anyway, that woods is an impossible tangle. I'm afraid I'll have to have it cleared."

The doctor made arrangements for Ann Marie to be taken to the hospital, where treatment for lockjaw and rabies would be started just to be on the safe side.

Sissie and Lotus were confined to the house for observation. The veterinarian who came to examine them Monday morning said that both dogs seemed to be in perfect health but that close observation would be necessary. Any signs of illness were to be reported immediately.

Monday afternoon Gil Dalton received a call from Mr. Neville's lawyer. Suit was being brought for negligence and for keeping a vicious animal. Damages up to $10,000, depending on the effects of the bite on the child's health, would be sought.

Gil was shocked. In order to pay $10,000, he would lose his home and savings. That would end his dream of starting High Point Kennels. When he told Jan about the lawsuit, they were both engulfed by gloom.

Nevertheless, the truth was that Sissie *had* trespassed on Mr. Neville's land.

On the Sunday that Ann Marie was bitten, the little girl had called Sissie out of the yard.

"Come on, Sissie," she whispered to her not unwilling cohort, and together child and dog scooted around to the forbidden thicket. Sissie loved the woods. The thick weeds and shrubs, the stirring of young animals, the singing of birds — all stirred Sissie's primitive longings to explore.

Ann Marie kept to a narrow path while Sissie raced ahead, returned to prance around Ann Marie, then raced off again. They were having a wonderful time.

Ann Marie saw the strange animal first. Sissie, well ahead of Ann Marie on the path, heard the child talking, recognized the words "doggie, nice doggie," and ran back to be petted. The fierce, bushy-tailed animal that faced Sissie was a complete surprise. Sissie sniffed the strange, wild odor of the raccoon that stood squarely in front of four tiny raccoon babies, half buried in the brush at the side of the path. Then, recognizing the ferocity of a mother defending her brood, Sissie backed away respectfully. Ann Marie was not so lucky. She reached for one of the babies.

Sissie saw the outraged mother strike and heard Ann Marie's wail of pain. With a growl, Sissie rushed for the raccoon, but the creature was too fast. The raccoon darted off, leaving Sissie behind. Then Sissie followed the crying child to the Daltons' front yard, where Ann Marie's grandfather found her.

Sissie hated being quarantined. Nor could she forget the animal that had bitten her little friend. Because Sissie's confinement followed the incident with the strange beast, she felt that she must find it to punish the criminal that had hurt her playmate. She waited for an opportunity to escape.

The Daltons, needless to say, were crushed by the incident. Most serious of all, a child had been hurt. Also, Sissie's reputation as a Sheltie of sound temperament and gentleness was in jeopardy of being destroyed by Ann Marie's accusation. And if Mr. Neville won his lawsuit, Gil and Jan would lose their home and kennel.

Sissie, thoroughly miserable, spent the two weeks of her quarantine moping around the house and thinking about the enemy that had outwitted her.

On the last day of Sissie's quarantine, a Sunday, the weather was particularly beautiful, and Gil let the dogs run loose in the back yard with the gate securely fastened. Sissie was delighted with her newly regained freedom.

Suddenly, Sissie broke into excited, high-pitched barking and ran to the gate. Ann Marie had come to play. Gil ran toward the gate, but the Sheltie was too fast for him. Just as Ann Marie slipped the latch and let the gate swing open, Sissie darted through to freedom and hurtled full speed toward the woods.

"Sissie, *come!*" Gil shouted after her, running past a surprised Ann Marie toward the thicket.

So intent was Sissie on her mission that she didn't hear Gil's command. Once in the wild zone, she stalked silent, a true hunter. Picking up the scent immediately, Sissie followed the trail to a stunted tree near the center of the thicket. A sudden flash of bushy, ringed tail revealed Sissie's enemy in the crotch of the tree about five feet from the ground. The raccoon was treed. As though she were a hunting dog, Sissie gave voice, barking as loud as she could.

Enraged, the raccoon sidled further out onto the thick branch and challenged Sissie with flashing, ringed eyes. She was in her natural habitat; the noisy intruder was not. The raccoon knew that she was safe in the tree.

When Gil caught up with Sissie, he was so angry and out of breath that he was ready to give the disobedient Sheltie a good thrashing. But Sissie's excited leaping about the tree trunk made him look up into the branches, where he saw not only the raccoon at bay, but the furry babies as well. He was puzzled.

"Sissie, shame on you," he scolded, "trying to attack a mother raccoon and her babies."

Sissie knew that Gil was angry. Her sad, brown eyes begged for forgiveness and understanding.

The arrival of Mr. Neville with Ann Marie sent Sissie slinking behind Gil's legs for protection, for Mr. Neville was an even more ferocious adversary than the raccoon. The old man's eyes squinted with fury.

"That settles it," he growled at Gil. "I've been much too easy with you and that vicious dog. I'm going to call the police and have you arrested for trespassing and for harboring a vicious animal."

He paused to get his breath. *"Now get off my property!"*

Heartsick to think that Sissie had bitten a child, Gil picked up the offending Sheltie and turned to carry the criminal home. Ann Marie blocked his path, crying hysterically.

"Don't worry, Ann Marie," Gil tried to soothe her. "Sissie won't hurt you again."

"Not Sissie, *that* doggie," Ann Marie shrieked. "There, up *there*." And she pointed to the now vacant branch where the raccoon had been a few seconds before.

"I wanted one of the little puppies to play with. I tried to get one, and the mother doggie bit me," Ann Marie explained.

Above in the tree, the ringed tail twitched angrily as the mother raccoon defied anyone to attack her young.

Mr. Neville was convinced. Sissie had been cleared.

'I'm sorry I doubted you, Sissie," Gil apologized later, sitting on the den couch while Sissie stretched out at his feet.

But he could see in Sissie's loving gaze that she had nothing to forgive him for. She had never lost faith in him. Gil felt ashamed until Sissie's tail thumping happily against his foot reminded him that everything had turned out just fine.

5

The Winner

All that spring, Gil and Jan Dalton became increasingly disturbed by the rivalry between Sissie and Lotus. They didn't want two feuding dogs in their household and began to fear that they would have to give up one of the dogs.

"Even if we *do* get the kennel name we want, and even if we *can* keep up the payments on High Point, how can we start a kennel with two female dogs that are ready to tear each other apart?"

As Jan complained to Gil, she slumped in despair, her hands jammed into her jeans pockets, her usually neat caramel-colored hair straggling down over her eyes.

Gil offered the obvious solution.

"If the girls can't get along, we'll have to sell one of them."

That morning Jan had given each dog a rawhide bone. Lotus immediately began to gnaw on hers, but growled when Sissie started to chew on her own bone. Sissie backed away, for Lotus could always send her daughter sprawling if she tried. Surrendering her bone to Lotus, Sissie started to walk away, but suddenly a black whirlwind whipped her onto her side. Lotus stood over her with white fangs gleaming. When Jan came to the rescue with a folded newspaper, Lotus reluctantly slunk back to her bone.

The Daltons were tired of that kind of bickering. But which one would they get rid of? They watched Sissie closely to see how she would develop.

And Sissie was blossoming at last. Short-coated and leggy at the beginning of winter, she hadn't looked like a show dog. But slowly her body had become graceful and well proportioned, and, most important, her coat had grown so that she now looked like a miniature collie — rough-coated, strong, yet elegant and alert.

"I think I know how to decide which to keep," Gil announced one warm spring day as he opened the mail.

He showed Jan the entry form for the Riverdale Shetland Sheepdog Specialty Show, which would be held early in June.

"You mean show both dogs and see if one of them wins? And keep the winner?" Jan read his mind.

"Well, the show might help us to decide."

So it was agreed, and the entries were mailed.

The day before the show, both Shelties were bathed, brushed, fluffed, and trimmed. Sissie loved all the attention.

Early on show day Lotus and Sissie hopped into the back seat of the station wagon. At first Lotus eyed Sissie with ill-concealed hostility and Sissie panted nervously, but in the excitement of this adventure, the two dogs felt drawn together and lay closer beside each other than they had for sometime.

Because this was a Shetland Sheepdog Specialty, only Shelties were to be shown. Scattered over the spacious green grounds were Shelties of all colors: sables ranging from pale gold to deep mahogany; flashy black Shelties like Lotus with tan and white markings; exotic blue merles, their gray coats mottled with black and tan. Handlers busily brushed and fluffed their charges.

As soon as the judging of the females began, Gil gave Lotus and Sissie a final brushing, slipped their show leads about their necks, and led them to ringside.

Sissie was to be judged first. Only two dogs were in the Novice Class, Sissie and a pale gold, delicate Sheltie. The judge examined the pale dog thoroughly, while her handler kept the dog alert and posing by holding out a bit of liver.

At the judge's command, the pale Sheltie trotted smoothly beside her handler. The crowd seemed to like her.

Then it was Sissie's turn to be looked at. Gil watched intently from ringside while Jan posed Sissie for the judge.

Skillfully, Jan set Sissie in the pose that would show off her natural beauty to best advantage. Sissie's russet coat gleamed like bronze, her white ruff and collar a dramatic contrast. She looked solid and strong but agile, with a finely sculptured head tapering to a firmly rounded muzzle.

Then, eager to show off, Sissie stepped out proudly beside Jan. Jan had to jog to keep up with her.

Finally, Sissie was placed beside the pale Sheltie while the judge compared the two dogs. He laid his hand on Sissie's head, and the contest was over. Sissie had won her class. The spectators' applause made Sissie wag all over with happiness.

"Sissie's a winner already," Jan said joyfully, handing Sissie's blue ribbon to Gil.

Next it was Lotus's turn to try to win her class. Gil rumpled Sissie's ears gently while Lotus, gleaming like ebony, trotted along with Jan into the ring for Open Class, in which the older, mature dogs would compete.

The judge signaled the ten handlers to gait their dogs in a circle while he studied the dogs' general appearance and movement. Then he examined each dog. The spectators watched silently.

With Sissie resting at his feet, Gil watched Jan show Lotus just as carefully as she had shown Sissie earlier. Since Lotus's failure to win now could mean that she might be sold, he had mixed emotions.

Finally, the judge waved four dogs, Lotus among them, to one end of the ring. This was a crucial moment. The winner would be selected from these four.

The sable next to Lotus stood haughty and arrogant, but she was nervous, and when the judge tried to examine her teeth, she shied away. The other sable bitch, a small, stocky matron still out of coat from her last litter, was a sound Sheltie. The fourth was a large blue merle Sheltie with a luxuriant coat and dazzling blue eyes.

After the judge felt the fragile bone structure underneath the gorgeous silver blue coat, he gestured the blue merle to third place. The nervous sable was fourth.

Now Lotus and the small, stocky sable stood together. Lotus held her head high and proud as if sensing the importance of looking her best. The onlookers watched expectantly.

When the judge motioned Lotus to first place, the crowd applauded enthusiastically. Jan hugged Lotus and led her to the winner's spot to receive her blue ribbon and a spectacular silver trophy. At ringside, Gil smiled happily. Now both Sissie and Lotus were winners.

Then the winners of all classes for females were called to the ring to compete for Winners title and championship points.

"It's between the young sable and the tricolor," someone said.

"They're mother and daughter," was one surprised comment.

"Looks like the daughter might give her mother some competition," said a veteran breeder.

In the ring, Gil and Jan smiled at the strangeness of the situation. Both knew that the real contest was between Lotus and Sissie.

Side by side, the rivals posed for the judge. Sissie was strong, young, eager; Lotus was lighter boned, graceful, and mature. It was an old story — the freshness of youth versus experienced maturity.

At ringside someone coughed, and a mother hushed a noisy child. The strain of the long contest showed in Jan's forced smile. The dogs also felt the strain of the contest.

Then, with a final glance at the two dogs, the judge pointed to Lotus. Lotus had won the coveted three points toward the title of Champion.

Proudly, Jan accepted the purple Winners ribbon and another handsome trophy. But the dogs' rivalry clouded her triumph.

"Well," she said on the way home, "Lotus was the winner. That means we sell Sissie."

There was a long silence.

"But Sissie was a winner, too," Gil pleaded. "She won her class, and she's just a year old. Think how terrific she'll be when she's as old as Lotus."

It was clear that the question of which dog to keep would not be solved easily. Lotus and Sissie, both winners, relaxed on the back seat, too tired to bicker with each other, happy to be going home.

6

To Catch A Thief

That summer Gil started giving Sissie obedience lessons. Sissie quickly learned the basic commands of sit, down, stay, and come. But her favorite lesson was retrieving. When Gil threw an old leather glove, Sissie would dash after it, snatch up the soft, familiar-scented glove, and gallop back to Gil to be praised. Her brown eyes sparkled with joy when Gil made a fuss over her.

Soon Sissie wanted to retrieve every object that was not too big or nailed down. When Jan threw away an old lamp shade, Sissie knocked over the trash can, dragged the battered shade to the back door, and barked, waiting for Jan to praise her. Sissie was disappointed that time.

Thereafter, trash was placed in a tightly covered container. Nevertheless, a strange assortment of twigs, old bones, and clothespins littered the back stoop daily as Sissie fetched presents to Jan and Gil.

During most of that summer, Sissie and Lotus, too warm to quarrel, just lazed on the patio or sprawled in the cool grass beneath the maple tree. Sissie's morning and evening lessons were followed by romps with Gil. Sissie was happy. It was a pleasant and uneventful summer — except for the burglaries.

Three homes near the Daltons were robbed of silver, jewelry, and furs while the owners were on vacation. There were no witnesses, and the police were stumped.

When Mr. and Mrs. Neville, their neighbors, left for a week's vacation in northern Wisconsin, the Daltons readily agreed to "keep an eye on things" for them.

The days passed uneventfully. Sissie became expert at retrieving and was still fetching odd gifts. Jan would laugh when Sissie bounded up with an old bone or a pair of Gil's shorts that had blown off the line. Gil was not so amused and, in fact, didn't like this new game. But since Sissie's "presents" seemed harmless, he did nothing to discourage her fun.

One day Sissie hit the jackpot.

That day Jan had several errands to do and, in her rush to get started, left the dogs outside. The Shelties loved to be out and had plenty of shade and fresh water to keep them comfortable. But Sissie got bored. When the cleaner's truck drove up, she didn't even bark at the familiar deliveryman, the same one who had once left the gate open at the old house. Finding no one home, the man opened the gate and hung Gil's suit on the screen door. When he turned to leave, the dogs were gone. He had done it again! Afraid of losing his job, the driver got into his truck and barreled out of the driveway.

But Sissie and Lotus were not runaways in the usual sense; they were simply restless. So off they went, exploring neighbors' yards, chasing cats, and having a good time. When they got tired and thirsty, they meandered home and sprawled under the maple tree to rest.

When Jan returned, Sissie danced impatiently around her.

"Sissie," Jan exclaimed, astonished at what she saw on the patio. "What have you been up to?"

On the patio lay Sissie's latest present to Jan — a mink scarf. Curled up like a living animal, little mink face staring sightless out of glass eyes, the pelt glistened in the sunlight like oiled teak. Though old-fashioned in style, the scarf was in excellent condition. While Jan examined the fur, Sissie wagged her tail, expecting praise.

But Jan frowned and did not praise her.

"Sissie, where did you get this?" Jan asked, as if expecting a reply. Sissie wagged her tail harder.

Then Jan saw the suit hanging on the screen door, noticed the unlocked gate, and thought that she knew what had happened. Sheepishly, she called the cleaner to ask if a mink scarf was missing from the truck. The cleaning company knew nothing; Jan had a real mystery on her hands.

Gil shared her bewilderment. The pelt obviously had not been thrown away because it was in perfect condition. Had Sissie stolen it? But *how?* Valuable furs were not left lying around.

They watched the lost-and-found ads for a few days, but none for a lost mink scarf appeared. Then Gil advertised, "Found, valuable apparel, can be claimed by owner on identification." Many people tried to claim the "valuable apparel," but none could identify the scarf.

Two days later, the Nevilles returned from their trip. Shortly after they arrived home, Mr. Neville ran puffing into the Daltons' living room.

"Welcome ho..." Gil began before Mr. Neville cut him short.

"Never mind all that," Mr. Neville sputtered. "Did you know that my house has been ransacked?" He paused to get his breath. "A fine job you did of 'keeping an eye on things.' Or did you pull the job yourself?"

"Now just a minute," Gil tried to calm the old man. "Come in and tell us exactly what happened."

"I don't know what happened," he snapped. "All I know is that my solid gold paperweight is gone, my father's watch, some jewelry of Emma's, and her mink scarf."

"Emma's what?" Jan interrupted.

"Oh, you know," Mr. Neville said impatiently, "one of those mink things with the beady eyes."

"Like this one?" Jan asked, holding up the scarf that Sissie had "fetched" home.

"Here, let me see that." Mr. Neville put on his glasses and examined the fur silently.

"This is my wife's fur," he said finally. "See, here are her initials embroidered on the underside, E.N. Would you mind telling me where you got it?"

The Daltons just stared at him. They didn't know what to say.

"Well?" asked Mr. Neville, his nose puckered with impatience.

"Why, uh, well, you see," Gil stammered.

"Where did you get my wife's fur?" their neighbor thundered.

"Sissie found it," Jan blurted out.

"Sissie...*what?*" Now it was Mr. Neville's turn to stare speechless.

"You see, Mr. Neville, Sissie got out of the yard the other day and brought the fur home. At least we think she did. We don't know where she found it, but obviously she couldn't have taken it from your house. Someone must have dropped it or thrown it away." Jan stopped, realizing that she wasn't making sense.

"Dropped it? Thrown it away? Are you all crazy? And what about the rest of my valuables? Did Sissie take them, too? And pick my lock in the bargain?"

His face red as a watermelon, Mr. Neville turned to go.

"I'm going to call the police," he said. "I don't know what's going on around here, but if you or that dog is responsible for my house being robbed, I'll prosecute. In the meantime, maybe I can recover the rest of my valuables. Or maybe Sissie can."

At mention of her name, Sissie wagged her tail, completely unaware of the crisis that she had created. Mr. Neville only scowled.

That evening Gil gave Sissie her lesson as usual. In the refreshing coolness, the eager Sheltie bounded happily after a wooden dumbbell. Twice Gil threw it, and twice Sissie retrieved it. On the third throw, however, instead of fetching the dumbbell, Sissie trotted to a corner of the garden and started digging.

"Sissie, what are you doing?" Gil scolded.

But before he could reach her, Sissie loped toward him carrying something shiny. She sat in front of Gil, offering him this delectable new object that was so much nicer than the awkward wooden dumbbell.

Without its coating of dirt, the object turned out to be a man's wristwatch, very old, with an inscription on the back: "To my son John," signed "R. Neville." The watch was a valuable heirloom.

"Sissie, where did you find this?" Gil asked as if Sissie could understand him and answer him. "Where did you find it?"

Sissie listened attentively. She knew the word "find."

Gil had taught her to track down articles by first giving her the scent and then sending her to find the object. So when Gil held the watch under Sissie's nose and said, "Where did you find it?" Sissie ran excitedly to the gate.

Gil suddenly realized that he had given her a command.

"It's worth trying," he muttered. He fastened Sissie's leash to her collar, let her sniff the watch again, and repeated the command "find it!" Sissie strained against her leash, and they started off.

She chose a twisted route. Often she doubled back on herself, sniffing furiously for a moment, then rushing on. Gil began to feel that he was on a wild-goose chase.

Once again he let Sissie smell the watch.

"Sissie, find it!" he repeated firmly. Sissie led him to a field on the other side of the highway. Sissie panted heavily now, and Gil was equally hot and tired. It was beginning to get dark. Mosquitos began to hunt.

"All right, Sissie," he said, unsnapping the leash, "you can explore the field for a few minutes. I suspect that's what you wanted all along."

Off leash, Sissie sniffed urgently in a zigzag pattern, progressing steadily toward the road. When she reached the open end of a huge drainpipe that extended underneath the highway, she barked excitedly until Gil joined her in the thick weeds around the opening. Gil peered inside but saw nothing.

"Sissie, let's go home," he ordered, tired and disgusted at wasting so much time and effort. But Sissie had disappeared.

"Sissie!" Gil called in a no-nonsense tone.

Out of the drainpipe crawled something weird. A bronze and white Sheltie, rumpled and cobwebby, bellied out of the pipe dragging a silver fox stole encased in a plastic bag.

Sissie wagged her tail proudly. What a wonderful present she had fetched. And this time Gil praised her generously.

A thorough search of the pipe by police disclosed watches, small fur pieces, and jewelry, all carefully bagged in plastic.

"Looks like a temporary hiding place," the police sergeant said. "I don't think an experienced thief would take a chance of getting his loot flooded out. We'll stake out the spot and wait until they come back."

"It was Sissie who tracked down the hiding place," Jan said, eager to have the Sheltie's efforts recognized. "She got loose one day and brought home a mink scarf that belonged to the...."

"You know," the sergeant interrupted with mock sternness, "it's against the law for a dog to run loose."

Jan blushed and shut up. At the same time, she hugged Sissie and had her face licked in return.

The stakeout worked. In a few days, two young burglars returned for their loot and were welcomed by police. Everyone got their valuables back, and no more robberies occurred in the neighborhood that summer.

Sissie had ended the crime wave.

7

A Trick or Two

"I could just scream!" wailed Jan after opening an official-looking letter from the American Kennel Club.

"What's the bad news?" Gil's voice was light, but his mouth held a stoic line.

"It seems there's a kennel in Ohio called Hi-Point English Setters. That could stand in the way of approval for High Point."

"Face it, Jan, if the name isn't approved, we'll just have to pick another. After all, it's the quality of dogs that we raise that matters, not the kennel name."

"I know, but I had my heart set on High Point. It's so symbolic of what we're working for. And we've already used the name in Sissie's registration — Sissie of High Point."

The mail held something more pleasant than the AKC letter — an invitation to spend a weekend at their friends', the Raymonds', lake cottage. Sissie was included in the invitation because the Raymonds thought that the Sheltie would be a good companion for their ten-year-old son.

For Bart Raymond was a problem. As the only child of well-to-do parents, he hadn't developed self-reliance; he depended on people around him to entertain him. Knowing that Bart wouldn't leave them alone with their guests, his parents innocently thought that Sissie would answer the boy's need for a playmate.

They left on a gorgeous July day with the Midwest sky a royal blue sea full of bobbing marshmallow clouds. Happy to be going along, Sissie leaped eagerly into the back of the station wagon onto her yellow shag rug. Sissie always preferred going along to being left at home. Lotus was in a boarding kennel for the weekend.

The "cottage" turned out to be a sizeable house with a private beach and a narrow wharf or dock. Evergreens and giant oaks grew abundantly on the beautiful grounds that sloped gently downward from the house to the lake.

After lunch, Gil and Jan, with Sissie trotting happily beside them, were given a tour of the grounds, starting at the house and ending at the dock. The lake, a green foil mirror, stretched nearly out of sight, with only a faint blur of trees indicating the far side.

At the shore, Sissie had a wonderful time investigating the new smells of algae, dead fish, and the lake itself, which she sniffed cautiously over the edge of the dock. Fascinated, she watched water bugs etch designs on the green glass of the lake's surface.

A loud plop in the water just a few feet from the wharf doused them all and set Sissie to barking loudly.

"What in the world...." began Mr. Raymond.

Whop! He didn't get a chance to finish. A large, flat rock sailed out of the bushes in front of the beach house and smacked the water, thoroughly splashing the four people and the bronze Sheltie standing on the wharf.

That was Sissie's introduction to Bart Raymond.

Bored as usual and resentful of the guests who were taking his parents' attention away from him, Bart had decided to ambush the visitors. When he saw the Sheltie, however, he crept out of the bushes.

"Here's our boy," Mr. Raymond beamed. "Come along, Bart, meet our guests. And just see what a nice dog they've brought along for you to play with."

Jan, her damp slacks clinging to her legs, began to doubt the wisdom of bringing Sissie.

Her fears were justified. Bart, a thin, wiry child, darted onto the wharf and grabbed for the dog's ruff. Sissie nimbly stepped aside, gliding in front of Jan to protect her from possible attack.

Bart couldn't check his rush. Over the edge of the dock he went! This time the splash that dampened their clothes made Gil and Jan smile. But when Bart squawked and spluttered helplessly, they realized, amazed, that he couldn't swim.

"I'm drowning, I'm drowning," Bart gasped.

Gil jumped into the lake, feet first, Sissie after him. He was astonished to find himself in less than four feet of water clouded by murky algae. Bart easily could have walked to shore.

"Boys will be boys," explained Mr. Raymond, mildly embarrassed.

Jan smiled politely at her host.

But Sissie was enjoying her first swim. She splashed and swam until she tired, then clambered onto shore, shaking repeatedly to dry herself.

Bart glared angrily at Sissie, blaming her for making him topple off the dock. Although he had turned the incident into a joke on the visitors, he remained furious at the Sheltie.

After everyone had changed into dry clothes, Gil put Sissie through her obedience lessons. The Raymonds applauded Sissie's sharp performance.

That is, everyone applauded but Bart. After showing mild interest at first, he quickly became bored when attention wasn't being paid to him.

"Can't Sissie do any tricks? Like sitting up and begging or dancing on her hind legs or jumping through a fiery hoop? Can't she do any really good tricks?"

"Sissie doesn't do tricks, Bart," Gil explained. "She's trained to do useful things, like retrieving, which make her a good companion."

"Oh, I thought she could do something really special," he said with exaggerated disappointment. "Mom and Dad said Sissie'd be fun to play with. She isn't." Then he ambled off toward the beach.

"He doesn't know much about dogs," Mr. Raymond apologized.

"He doesn't know much about manners either," Jan whispered to Gil later.

Unaware of the undercurrent of tension, Sissie was enjoying herself immensely. Here was all the freedom and wide open space that any dog could desire.

Later Bart seemed sorry and asked to help prepare Sissie's dinner. Gil showed him how to moisten the dry dog food and mix it with meat scraps. The boy seemed eager to help.

When Sissie began to eat, however, she suddenly stepped back from her bowl in anger and surprise. She growled and jiggled the bowl with her paw.

"Doesn't Sissie like her dinner?" Bart asked innocently.

Gil investigated. A large night crawler wiggled through Sissie's bowl! Gil had no doubt about how it got there, but Bart just looked the other way and whistled.

After dinner, Bart asked to take Sissie for a walk. Gil hesitated to entrust Sissie to the mischievous boy, but the Raymonds wanted to play bridge and didn't want Bart to annoy them. So Gil fastened a leather leash to Sissie's collar and handed the leash to Bart.

Bart jerked the leash hard. Sissie was puzzled — no one had given her a command. Questioningly, she looked up at Gil and then at the boy who scowled darkly at her.

"No, no!" Gil protested, struggling to control his temper. "Let me show you how to get her to heel. First, you — "

He didn't have a chance to finish, because with Sissie dashing along beside him to avoid being jerked, Bart ran as fast as he could toward the beach.

"Oh, come on, let's play cards. Boys and dogs always get along together, everyone knows that. You don't have to worry."

Out of politeness and a sincere desire to believe that Bart meant well, Gil agreed to play cards and let Bart and Sissie go. Jan consented reluctantly.

But Sissie was in trouble.

Determined to make her miserable, Bart jerked the leash harshly until Sissie was entirely mystified. Patiently, she suffered the boy's abuse.

"How about a boat ride, Sissie?" Bart asked, leading the Sheltie onto the dock toward the moored rowboat.

"Jump in, that's a good dog," he said pleasantly.

Happy to be finally pleasing this strange master, Sissie hopped obediently into the boat. It rocked slightly. Then Bart leaned over and looped Sissie's leash around one of the seats and tied it securely. Sissie whined at Bart to untie her, but no such luck. Then Bart stooped to shove the boat and its prisoner out into the lake. In his zeal to punish the little Sheltie that had embarrassed him this afternoon, however, he pushed a little too hard. As his hands left the side of the boat, he lost his balance and fell into the boat headfirst.

The impact of Bart's body tumbling into the boat combined with the shove that the boy had given sent the small craft leaping into the lake, where, caught by a mild current, it drifted away from shore. Although Bart moaned a few times, not for half an hour did he open his eyes. Sissie was licking his face. His head ached, and at first he didn't fully realize what had happened.

When Bart finally sat up and looked around, it was getting dark, and the boat had drifted to just about the center of the slate-colored lake. Sissie licked away a small bloodstain on Bart's forehead, then, determined to free herself, she set about gnawing through the leash that tied her to the boat.

"OK, Sissie, I might as well untie you," Bart said weakly as he unfastened the leash. "I've goofed the whole thing anyhow. And oh, my head!"

Feeling queasy, Bart slumped to the floor of the rowboat. All he had to do was wait to be found.

Sudden fear made him sit up straight. Why would he be found? His parents were playing bridge, a game that often occupied them for hours. When would they look for him? In a few hours? Would they even notice that the boat was gone? Could they find him at night? Bart shivered from terror and cold as darkness shut him off from safety. Shouting for help only made him hoarse, with no result. Sissie whined sympathetically.

In panic, Bart seized the oars that lay on the bottom of the boat, but the clumsy oars were hard for the injured boy to handle. One oar slipped out of his fingers and drifted away into the blackness.

Bart began to cry. Sissie, licking away the tears, snuggled close to the despairing boy, herself uneasy and uncertain of how to get back to shore.

Sissie stood up in the boat and stretched her cramped legs; then she sniffed in all directions. Steadily, the boat continued to drift, but the wind was rising now, and the boat began to rock.

For a moment Sissie stood perfectly still as if trying to reach a decision. Then she leaped out of the boat and swam in the direction of the drifting oar.

"Sissie, come back," Bart called after her, not wanting to be left alone and fearing that Sissie would drown. Now that he and Sissie had been literally in the same boat, he felt an affection for her that he had been unable to feel earlier. But it was too late. Sissie was gone. Bart was alone in the boat adrift on the lake — the very fate that he had planned for the sable Sheltie.

Sissie had not acted without purpose. As the boat steadily drifted toward the opposite shore, the hungry Sheltie smelled food cooking. It was toward civilization and help that she swam. Because she wasn't a seasoned swimmer, her progress was slow, but eventually she emerged, wet and shivering. After shaking herself vigorously, she headed for the nearest cottage and scratched at the door. It opened. Soon people surrounded her, drying her with rough towels, examining her collar, and making clucking sounds about the poor, lost, half-drowned "collie pup."

Sissie's collar bore an address over one hundred miles away. Surely the dog hadn't wandered *that* far from home. Nevertheless, Sissie's benefactors called the phone number on the collar. There was no answer.

Sissie, meanwhile, with unfinished business out on the lake, whined urgently and leaped against the door repeatedly.

"Why, she wants to get out again," a young girl said, "and after she was so glad to get in. Something must be wrong out there."

"Maybe she just wants to go home," the boy said.

They decided to let Sissie have her way. The boy grabbed a flashlight, and he and his sister followed Sissie to the shore, where the boy shone his flashlight into the darkness over the rippling black water. Sissie barked excitedly all the while.

"Dad," the boy called to the man inside the house, "we'd better get out the boat. Looks like trouble on the lake."

From their boat, the boy and his father spotted Bart, weak with fear and exhaustion and suffering from seasickness. After they had put the boy to bed, his rescuers called the Raymonds, who were stunned to hear what was happening to their son while they were winning at bridge. Sissie stayed close to Bart, licking the pale hand that weakly stroked her head and rumpled her ears.

Later that night, the Raymonds arrived by car with the Daltons. A doctor declared Bart fine except for an ugly bump and cut on his forehead. But he needed rest. His rescuers and new friends said good-bye and promised to visit him in a few days.

"We had a rough crossing, Sissie and I," Bart explained drowsily as his relieved parents made him comfortable on the back seat of the station wagon.

"But I wasn't worried a minute," he said, hugging Sissie as the Sheltie snuggled close to him on the seat.

"You see," he said, smiling, "Sissie knew a trick or two after all."

8

A Day in Court

The Daltons could hardly believe it — someone had called the police and reported Sissie as a public nuisance. The anonymous caller referred to a local ordinance making a dog's "undue and excessive barking" a crime. The Daltons were notified that a formal complaint had been filed against them.

This is the way it came about.

The house to the left of the Daltons had been sold recently, and the new owners were not sympathetic to dogs. The Weigles had one son, a boy about twelve who had been crippled from birth and could not walk without crutches. Mark, a pale, thin boy with large hazel eyes and long black lashes, loved dogs and watched longingly at the fence while Sissie was having her lessons. His overprotective parents, however, insisted that he stay away from the "dirty" animals that "might bite you and knock you down." Nevertheless, Mark was fascinated by Sissie.

The Daltons felt sorry for Mark because he seemed so lonely. The tutor who came to teach him everyday was no substitute for the boys and girls of a regular school. Mark felt "different" and set apart from children his own age. He lived in virtual isolation.

Sissie liked the frail boy, who watched quietly at the fence while she retrieved for Gil and jumped over hurdles. When she knew that Mark was watching her, she did especially well.

After her lesson, Sissie would dash over to the fence, leap against it, and squeeze her nose between the wire mesh, wagging her tail happily. Timidly, Mark would extend his pale fingers to be licked. The two became friends.

One Saturday morning, Gil invited Mark to come over and watch Sissie's training close up. Mark was ecstatic. With great difficulty, he made his way to Sissie's yard, then perched on a redwood bench while Sissie sailed through her jumping and retrieving beautifully.

When Gil asked Mark if he would like to give Sissie some commands, Mark eagerly agreed. Supporting himself on his crutches, he stood up and took the dumbbell from Gil.

"Sissie, heel," Mark commanded, and although Sissie was a little confused at first because of the crutches and Mark's limping gait, she assumed heel position at Mark's left side. Then Mark threw the dumbbell.

"Sissie, fetch!" he ordered.

Sissie flew after the dumbbell and galloped back to Mark. Squarely in front of him, she sat waiting for him to take it, but this was not easy for Mark to do. First, he shifted his weight to the withered leg that was supported by a heavy steel brace. Then, steadying himself against his crutch, he managed to reach down far enough to grasp the dumbbell from Sissie's jaws.

"Sissie, heel," he said, and Sissie finished smartly at the heel position.

Mark praised Sissie lavishly, overjoyed that he actually had participated in Sissie's training instead of being just a spectator. Never before had he thought that he could train a dog himself. He grinned triumphantly.

Sissie, happy that she had pleased her friend, licked his hand and leaped up against him, ready to play.

But after bending down to take the dumbbell from Sissie, Mark had trouble regaining his balance. The weight of the eighteen-pound dog jumping playfully against him was enough to send the frail boy sprawling, crutches and all, before Gil could reach him.

This was the scene that Mr. Weigle, Mark's father, saw as he came looking for his son: the boy sprawled helplessly on the ground, his crutches lying out of his reach, and a russet and white Sheltie doing something to the boy's face.

With a shout, Mr. Weigle reached his son and aimed a kick at Sissie, who was sympathetically licking Mark's cheek.

"Just a minute!" Gil Dalton shouted, stepping in front of Sissie. "It was an accident. Mark's all right. He'll know what to expect of Sissie now and won't be caught off guard again. He was having a great time, Mr. Weigle, he has a way with dogs. Besides — "

Gil was interrupted by a stream of insults as Mr. Weigle picked up his protesting son and carried him home as he would a baby.

"It's a shame," said Jan, who had watched the incident from

the kitchen window. "The boy gets so much enjoyment playing with Sissie. He needs to have fun. And he needs to learn how to do things on his own. He'll either grow into an independent man someday or remain a hopeless cripple."

"Well, I certainly won't invite Mark over again without his parents' consent," said Gil. "And Mr. Weigle isn't likely to give it."

"Perhaps Mrs. Weigle will be easier to convince," said Jan. "I was meaning to talk to her anyway about joining our neighborhood planning committee."

"Helping Mark is a lost cause as long as his father refuses to let him do things by himself," Gil concluded.

"We'll see," Jan replied with the hint of a plan in her voice.

But before Jan could talk to Mrs. Weigle, the police officer came to investigate a complaint of excessive barking. Lotus and Sissie did not help matters by barking furiously at the policeman, who was just an intruder to them.

"But we have so much ground here," Jan protested. "How could anyone possibly be annoyed by the barking?"

"The ordinance is not against people being annoyed by barking, Ma'am, it's against excessive barking, whether anyone gets bothered or not. As long as that kind of barking is going on, anyone has a right to complain."

"That just doesn't make sense," Jan argued. "That's like the old riddle about whether the tree falling in the forest makes a sound if nobody is around to hear it."

"I don't know anything about trees," the policman answered impatiently. "This barking offense carries an automatic fine of twenty-five dollars unless you want to appear in court to contest it."

And that was how matters now stood. The Daltons hated to pay the fine when no one had been really bothered by excessive barking. But if they went to court and were convicted, the judge might order the Daltons to get rid of their dogs. That would be a real blow to the two people who dearly loved their Shelties and hoped to found a kennel.

In spite of the risk, Gil decided to appear before the court, and a date was set for the hearing.

Jan, meanwhile, called on Mrs. Weigle, ostensibly about the neighborhood planning committee's annual rummage sale.

"We'd love to have Mark visit us," Jan said, after Mrs. Weigle had asked her to sit down. "Mark and Sissie seem to have become good friends."

A zigzag furrow formed along Mrs. Weigle's brow as she shook her head sadly.

"I know," she said. "Mark needs to get out more, needs friends his own age. But I can't convince his father. You see, Mark is our only child, and his father is afraid that something might hurt him. He is a frail boy."

"Of course," Jan replied sympathetically. "But we would watch him closely; we wouldn't let him fall again."

The result of the meeting was that Jan and Sue Weigle became friends, both secretly vowing to help Mark achieve more independence.

One evening soon afterward, Jan received a phone call from Sue Weigle. Mrs. Weigle felt ashamed, she said, that her husband had reported Sissie for excessive barking. She had just learned about the impending hearing and hoped that no harm would be done.

Jan thanked her for calling. Now that the anonymous accuser was identified, the Daltons felt better; at least they knew who their enemy was. With just five days until the hearing, they began in earnest to find people who would testify on Sissie's behalf. Mr. Weigle was notified of the proceedings and was ordered to attend. The Daltons had called his bluff.

The day of the hearing, Sissie accompanied Gil and Jan to court. Curiously, she sniffed the stuffy courtroom where the private hearing was to be held.

"Is this the accused?" asked the judge, pointing to Sissie.

"Yes, Your Honor," answered Jan. "She is here to be her own character witness."

The accused wagged her bronze and white plume of a tail.

First, Mr. Weigle was called to the bench. Bitterly, he told a story of a howling dog keeping him awake at night; a barking dog frightening his cat; a vicious dog threatening his son. It was a tale calculated to strike terror into the hearts of the listeners. The judge listened patiently, glancing occasionally at the slender bronze and white Sheltie lying quietly at Jan Dalton's feet.

"Is there any further testimony against the dog?" asked the judge, when Mr. Weigle had finished his tirade against Sissie.

"Why no, Your Honor," spluttered Mr. Weigle. "Mine should be enough. I'm an honest taxpayer and my word is good."

The defense witnesses were next. Mr. Neville testified how Sissie's barking had uncovered the raccoon that had bitten his granddaughter. Mrs. Raymond told about how Sissie's barking had led rescuers to her son Bart, stranded at night on the lake.

"Your Honor," Jan summed up the defense. "Mr. Neville

didn't consider excessive the barking that helped to save his granddaughter the pain of antirabies treatment. Mrs. Raymond's son was happy to hear Sissie's 'excessive barking.' What is 'excessive' barking anyway? If a burglar comes, should a dog bark twice and then curl up and go to sleep? Isn't constant, sustained barking necessary to bring help to an injured or lost child? How else can a dog communicate in a world full of noise and busy people?"

"But," said the judge, "there is a specific complaint against the dog in this case; namely, of undue noise and vicious behavior. Is it true that Sissie knocked Mark Weigle to the ground and then went for his throat?"

"Yes, Your Honor, it's true, it's true!" shouted Mr. Weigle, jumping up excitedly.

But just at that moment no one was paying much attention to Mr. Weigle. At the rear of the courtroom, a woman accompanied by a young boy wearing a leg brace and hobbling awkwardly on crutches entered and made their way slowly forward.

"Sue! Mark! What are you doing here?" Mr. Weigle asked harshly. "This is none of your affair."

Tight-lipped and determined, Mrs. Weigle stood before the judge.

"Your Honor," she said, "I live next door to the Daltons and have never been aware of excessive barking. Actually, the dogs do me a service by letting me know when deliverymen and salesmen are coming. And Sissie's done my boy here a world of good. Mark loves Sissie. He wouldn't love her if she were vicious, would he?"

"And one more thing, Judge," Mrs. Weigle continued in spite of her husband's scowls, "Sissie couldn't have frightened our cat because we don't have a cat!"

Breathless, flushing red with embarrassment, Sue Weigle paused a moment, then bravely continued.

"Your Honor, I think my husband's complaint was ill-advised," she said with conviction, then sat down.

"And what have you to say about all this, young man?" the judge addressed Mark.

"Sissie and I are friends, Sir," the worried boy replied. "Sissie's helped me a lot. We'd like to show you something if we could."

"We?" the judge asked patiently, as if aware that more was at stake here than a dog's barking.

"Me and Sissie, Your Honor. We'd like to show you how we work together."

The judge was willing, and a space was cleared in front of the bench. Then, while Mr. Weigle watched openmouthed, Jan handed Sissie's leash to Mark.

"Sissie, heel!" Mark commanded firmly, swinging forward awkwardly on his crutches, the end of Sissie's leash looped around the crutch. Sissie trotted obediently beside Mark, sitting whenever he halted, walking slowly to adapt to the boy's uneven gait. The two put on an amazing exhibition of dog-handler cooperation, each seeming to anticipate the next move of the other. Sissie performed as well as she ever had with Gil.

Then, while Sissie sat alertly beside him, Mark produced a dumbbell from his jacket pocket and threw it down the courtroom aisle.

"Sissie, fetch!" he ordered.

Sissie leaped to fetch the dumbbell, then brought it to Mark and sat in front of him, waiting for the boy to take it.

Mr. Weigle could sit still no longer.

"That's how Mark fell, trying to take that thing from the dog. He can't bend down like that, he — "

Here Mr. Weigle trailed off helplessly because Mark, by shifting his weight skillfully onto the braced leg, *was* bending down to take the dumbbell from Sissie's eager jaws. Then Sissie swung around to sit at Mark's left side. This time, moreover, when Mark praised her, she did not jump up against him. Instead, she licked his hand and pranced around the boy without bumping or jostling him.

"What is this, a conspiracy?" asked Mr. Weigle, not knowing whether to rejoice in his son's accomplishment or scold him for disobedience.

"Yes, a conspiracy," said Mrs. Weigle. "This is a conspiracy to help Mark become more self-sufficient. And I think he's doing just fine. We've been practicing — Mark, Sissie, and I — and Mark has been happier and livelier than he has ever been. He even wants to go to public school next semester, and I think we should let him."

A loud rap of a gavel interrupted her as the judge rose and said smiling, "Case dismissed. Court adjourned for lunch." On the way out, he stooped to give Sissie a pat on the head. Sissie wagged her tail at the kindly stranger.

Gil strode hastily over to Mr. Weigle and extended his hand.

"Won't you and Mrs. Weigle and Mark join us for lunch," he invited. "Maybe we can iron this out among ourselves. After all, we're neighbors."

Sheepishly, Bob Weigle shook hands with Gil Dalton and accepted his invitation.

"You know, Mark," the boy's father said at lunch in one of the city's finest restaurants, "maybe there's something to this dog training after all. How would you like to have a dog of your own to train and take care of? A Sheltie maybe?"

"*Would* I?" Mark exclaimed unbelievingly. Then he sobered. "Of course, it would have to be exactly like Sissie."

"We'll try to find one as much like Sissie as possible," his father promised. "In fact, Mr. Dalton, that is, Gil, told me that Lotus is expecting puppies."

Mark grinned happily at his father.

After lunch they all went home, good friends and neighbors. Sissie had had her day in court.

9

The Wonder Dog

Wagging her white-tipped plume of a tail, Sissie looked quizzically from one of her favorite people to the other. Gil and Jan Dalton talked excitedly, repeating Sissie's name often, which made the Sheltie wonder whether she was being praised or whether she was expected to obey some new command.

"It would be a unique opportunity for High Point Kennels to go international," Gil told his wife.

"But Japan," groaned Jan. "That's the other side of the world. We'd never see her again."

"But Sissie would be the foundation for a new line of Japanese Shelties if we sold her to Mr. Yoshido. She'd be famous."

"But she'd be gone!" cried Jan, horrified at the thought of losing Sissie. Sissie wagged her tail harder than ever.

"Come on, Sissie, let's get the mail," Jan invited her, and in spite of the sticky August heat, Sissie leaped and pranced around Jan all the way to the curbside mailbox. Although she was over one year old, Sissie still acted like a puppy.

"Not here yet," Jan sighed, disappointed with the mail. Sissie, sensing Jan's unhappiness, licked her owner's knee.

Back on the patio again, Sissie took a cool drink from her water bowl, then lay down near Lotus.

"Why is the American Kennel Club so slow about granting us our kennel name?" Jan complained.

"We just have to wait," Gil said stoically. "We have no other choice."

Jan frowned at the thought that their application might be refused. High Point Kennels had been a dream so long and was now nearly a reality. They had the grounds to house several dogs and two sound females to begin their new line of Shelties. Failure was not pleasant to think about.

A snarl turned the Daltons' attention to the dogs. Looking for a playmate, Sissie had tried to coax her mother into a game. But Lotus, expecting puppies, was grouchy and snapped at her lively daughter.

"There's another advantage to sending Sissie to Japan," Gil pointed out, watching the two dogs quarrel. "When Lotus has her puppies, those two are going to be scrapping all the time. If we send Sissie away, that problem will be solved."

"Maybe Lotus should go to Japan; she already has an oriental name," quipped Jan without humor.

"But it's Sissie that Mr. Yoshido saw at a dog show and liked."

The question of whether to sell Sissie was left hanging. It was too hot to decide. Besides, there was time yet. Mr. Yoshido planned to stay in the United States several weeks longer and would call them for their decision before he left.

Meanwhile, Gil continued training Sissie for obedience trial competition. At the Midvale Shetland Sheepdog Specialty the last Sunday in August, Sissie placed second to qualify for the first "leg" of her Companion Dog title. Gil was delighted with her score of 197. The following Sunday, she repeated with a second place win at Cambridge Dog Club and a score of 197½ out of a possible 200. Now she needed just one more qualifying score to complete her title. Gil decided to try to win Sissie's Companion Dog title at the Fox River Kennel Club's September show.

So interesting did Gil find obedience work that he had forgotten about showing Sissie in conformation. But something happened to change his attitude abruptly.

On Labor Day morning, a friend came to show the Daltons her new ten-month-old Sheltie, recently purchased for a huge price from Crestline Kennels.

Sissie and Lotus barked excitedly at the red-gold Sheltie, then wagged their tails and invited Heather to play.

"She's guaranteed," Jan's friend, Betty Stuart, said. "Absolutely guaranteed to win. Crestline said that Heather's the best puppy they've had in years. Heather's a once-in-a-lifetime Sheltie. She's a wonder dog."

Politely, Gil and Jan scrutinized their friend's puppy, and not without some envy, for Heather was a real beauty. She had a strong, graceful body, a finely molded head with a well-rounded muzzle and an amazingly abundant coat for a youngster. Her dark, almond-shaped eyes were set at just the right angle, and her ears tipped perfectly.

Sissie compared favorably with Heather, although Sissie was the color of burnished mahogany and was a little taller. Sissie had more of the collie's elegance and noble expression than did Heather, who seemed fragile in comparison. Sissie's eyes held a deep, mature expression in contrast to Heather's flighty gaze. But both dogs were beauties.

"I've got Heather entered in conformation at Fox Valley. Crestline thinks that she can win even though she's less than a year old," Betty Stuart boasted.

Her arrogance annoyed Gil. He disliked bragging. Moreover, he did not think that Heather was *that* good, and, especially, he did not like the idea of a kennel's guaranteeing that a dog would win.

"I'm going to show Sissie in conformation at Fox Valley, too," Gil announced to Jan's complete amazement, "as well as in obedience."

"But..." Jan began helplessly.

"Wonderful!" interrupted Betty. "I'll see you there. And may the better dog win."

"Why did you say that?" asked Jan after Betty had gone. "Sissie's coat isn't in top condition now. She's sure to lose. Why not just show her in obedience as you originally planned?"

"Sissie's every bit as good a Sheltie as Heather," Gil insisted. "She can hold her own with *that* bit of orange fluff."

"Well, just remember, it was your idea," said Jan.

Gil remained resolute, and Sissie was entered in both conformation and obedience at Fox Valley. There was no turning back now.

By show day, however, Gil was sorry that he had rashly entered Sissie in conformation. Early September was very hot, and Sissie continued to shed heavily. Moreover, the hot weather made her lose her appetite and she lost weight. Sissie was still beautiful, but definitely not in top show condition. The Daltons had one hope — probably none of the other Shelties would be in top shape either.

"Maybe we had better not go," suggested Gil.

"Remember, it was your idea to show Sissie in conformation," Jan reminded him in an I-told-you-so tone.

Gil had no defense. They went to the show as planned.

At Fox Valley, Gil groomed Sissie best as he could, rubbing white chalk powder into her ruff to give it body. It was no use. After the chalk was brushed out, Sissie's coat still looked skimpy.

Gil gave Sissie a final brushing. She was as ready as she would ever be.

Eager as usual to please Gil, Sissie trotted obediently beside him to the Sheltie ring. On the way they passed the trophy stand, where all the show prizes were displayed. Although he usually considered looking at trophies ahead of time bad luck, Gil felt compelled to stop and look at one trophy in particular — the Shetland Sheepdog Best of Breed award.

This trophy was a masterpiece of marble and walnut in three tiers. Two carved walnut columns rose fully three and one-half feet from a slab of white Italian marble, with a smaller marble slab at midheight and a yet smaller piece at the top. The top slab served as a platform for a gold-toned figure of a Sheltie. A gold plate at the base of the trophy would be engraved with the winner's name.

Beside the Best of Breed trophy stood a similar trophy, a replica in every detail except the crowning piece was a winged victory figure holding aloft the winner's precious laurel wreath.

Gil stared at the trophies for a minute, then continued with Sissie trotting happily beside him to the show ring where several other Shelties waited, none of them in any better coat than Sissie. So far, Sissie seemed well able to hold her own. Gil felt much better.

But just as the judging of the females was about to begin, all eyes turned toward one Sheltie being led to ringside. Breeders and handlers gaped with envy as the gorgeous, red-gold Sheltie danced to the ring, head high, dainty white forepaws arching as she pranced along. But the feature of the newcomer that really caused havoc was her coat. This dog had an incredible coat for this time of year. Next to the skimpy-coated Shelties at ringside, the red Sheltie's fluffy coat stood out as though she had just come from the North Pole. All the handlers frowned with wonder and despair.

Heather, the dog attracting all this attention, seemed to be having a wonderful time. With instinctive showmanship, she played to the crowd, arching her graceful neck, waving her plumed tail royally at her subjects, assuming easily and naturally an alert pose. Betty Stuart smiled with confidence.

"Did you see the Sheltie trophy?" Betty asked the Daltons.

Gil nodded longingly, thinking of the magnificent trophy so obviously out of his reach.

Sissie, wanting to play, ran up to Heather. The two dogs wagged their tails, but play would have to be postponed. The judge was ready.

Puppy and Novice classes were over quickly, and the judge was soon ready for Open, the really important class. With Betty Stuart and Heather close behind them, Gil led Sissie into the ring.

There was little doubt in anyone's mind about who would win the class, and when the judge handed the blue ribbon to Betty Stuart, the audience politely applauded. Sissie was second, and a tricolor placed third. Sissie had been beaten.

Outside the ring she licked Gil's hand, waiting to be petted and praised for her performance. But she was not praised. Even Jan looked glum and disapproving. Sissie couldn't understand what she had done wrong. From ringside, the Daltons watched Heather go on to receive the spectacular Best of Breed trophy. Betty Stuart smiled happily as she received her huge prize. This was a sensational win for such a young dog.

The Daltons congratulated Betty Stuart as she swept past them with the wonder dog, Heather.

"This may just be the end of Sissie's show career," Gil whispered to Jan.

Of course, Sissie could not know that Gil's pride was hurt at her having been defeated. Sissie did not even know what winning meant.

But she did know when Gil was unhappy with her. And both Gil and Jan were ignoring her as though they were angry. Miserable, Sissie curled up between Gil's feet, resting her head against his right shoe. Usually this brought a pat and a rumpling of Sissie's soft ears, but not today.

"Well, Sissie, maybe you can pass your obedience class today," Gil said without enthusiasm.

A brief warmup of heeling exercises made Sissie feel much better. At least Gil was paying her some attention. This time, however, in her desire to please, Sissie was a little too eager; she began to anticipate commands, that is, to sit or move before Gil gave her the command. Anticipating commands is a serious fault; Gil scolded her with a sharp jerk of the choke collar.

So eager was Sissie to please Gil that she didn't realize that she was doing anything wrong. When Gil jerked the leash, Sissie's spirits were crushed. She hung her head and plodded along beside Gil, her brown eyes full of misery. No matter how she tried, she could not seem to please Gil.

Gil realized his mistake immediately — the error of punishing a dog in anger. A light jerk of the collar would have been warning enough to Sissie that she was anticipating commands. Ashamed, Gil bent down and rumpled Sissie's silken ears in the usual way that she knew and loved.

"Good Sissie, good girl," Gil praised her with genuine affection in his voice. "You're worth more than any trophy, Sissie. What's more, you're not going to Japan. You're going to live your entire life with Jan and me. You're our dog."

Sissie wriggled all over with happiness. Although she didn't understand all the words, she knew by his tone that Gil loved her again. That was all Sissie wanted.

At ringside, watching Betty Stuart showing off her enormous trophy, Gil could not suppress a feeling of envy. How handsome that trophy would have looked on the old mahogany desk in the den. But Sissie had been beaten and that was that.

There was now only one dog ahead of Sissie in obedience. When the dog entered the ring, Gil was astounded — the dog was Heather! Was the wonder Sheltie to plague Sissie even in obedience? Gil wished more than ever that they had stayed home that day.

Sissie wagged her tail at Heather, ready to play. But Heather had work to do.

On leash, Heather's heeling deserved a near-perfect score. The crowd applauded. But when Betty Stuart took off Heather's leash, a transformation took place in the beautiful Sheltie.

"Heel!" Betty Stuart commanded Heather. Heather looked around, saw Sissie waiting for her turn in the ring, then bounded out of the ring and over to Sissie, ready to play. Horrified, Betty ran to leash her dog. But it was too late — Heather had been disqualified.

The Daltons were embarrassed. They felt it was their fault that Heather had run out of the ring; they should have kept Sissie out of sight until Heather had completed all the exercises. Now it was Betty Stuart's turn to look disappointed.

Sissie was next in the ring. Happy again, tail waving, Sissie heeled as though she were glued to Gil's left heel. No matter how sharply he halted, Sissie sat instantly. Off leash she did equally well. In all, Sissie gave a stunning performance of novice obedience work. She left the ring amid vigorous applause.

Later, when prizes were announced, Sissie had placed first. Gil could hardly believe that Sissie had done so well after such a poor practice session: the mahogany Sheltie had scored 199 points out of a possible 200 — almost a perfect score! For her victory, Sissie received a silver-plated tray, a much smaller trophy than the huge award that Heather had won. This time, at ringside, Sissie got all the praise and petting she wanted.

Feeling guilty, Gil apologized to Betty Stuart for Sissie's tempting Heather to run out of the ring. Otherwise, Gil admitted, Heather would probably have done just as well as Sissie.

"Of course she wouldn't have," Betty contradicted him. "She wouldn't even have qualified."

Gil was bewildered. Was Betty saying that Heather was not really a wonder dog after all?

"Wasn't it Sissie's fault that Heather ran out of the ring?" he asked again.

"Not at all. Heather simply wasn't ready for obedience competition. She's just a youngster, and I haven't worked with her nearly long enough for her to be as good as Sissie. I think that Heather will be a good obedience dog someday, but right now she's too young and flighty. Oh, she's pretty enough, but she's not dependable yet. No, Sissie had nothing to do with Heather's bolting out of the ring."

The Daltons, greatly relieved that Betty didn't blame them, began to see the day's events in a new light.

"You know," Betty continued, "even a wonder dog can only win when he's ready — when he's had the proper training or is in top condition. Sissie wasn't in good coat today, and Heather hadn't been trained long enough. A dog doesn't win just because his owner wants him to."

The wisdom of Betty Stuart's words struck home.

"Then Sissie is a wonder dog, too," said Jan, and they all laughed while Sissie and Heather wagged their tails as hard as they could.

Just then Gil was surprised to hear Sissie's number — 67 — called over the loudspeaker. Sissie was wanted in the obedience ring again. But why? Had she done something wrong after all and been disqualified? Soon Gil and Sissie stood alone with the judge in the center of the obedience ring. The spectators leaned forward, eager to find out what was going to happen next.

Then the judge presented Gil with a beautiful blue and gold rosette ribbon and a mate to the trophy that Heather had won, exact in all details except that instead of a Sheltie on top, a winged figure held high the victor's coveted laurel. On the base of the trophy was engraved "Highest Scoring Dog in Trial."

The spectators gave Sissie an enthusiastic round of applause. Then Gil and Jan hugged Sissie and admired the big trophy gleaming gold and burnished walnut and creamy marble in the light of photographers' flashbulbs. Sissie was a celebrity.

Best of all, this win meant that Sissie was now a Companion Dog, entitled to have the letters C.D. after her name. She had earned her first obedience title as well as two beautiful trophies.

Tired, happy, and much wiser, Gil and Jan Dalton took their wonder dog home.

* * * * *

On Tuesday, when Mr. Yoshido called to get the Daltons' verdict about selling Sissie, Gil told him what he and Jan had decided.

"Sissie may be a Champion some day, Mr. Yoshido, and maybe not, but she's a great obedience dog with a High in Trial

award already. And mainly, she's our dog, our pet. Sissie belongs with us. We sincerely don't believe she'd be happy anywhere else."

"I am sorry, but I understand your decision and respect your reasons," Mr. Yoshido told Gil.

"Sayonara, then," he added. "That means goodbye in Japanese."

"Sayonara, Mr. Yoshido. And thank you."

* * * *

On Wednesday, like an omen, the letter arrived from the American Kennel Club granting permission for the Daltons to officially use the name High Point Kennels, Registered, as long as they agreed never to breed English Setters.

That evening Jan and Gil toasted the official launching of their kennel with champagne. Then, with the dogs sprawled at their feet, they began to design their new kennel sign.

Gil kept glancing at Sissie's magnificent trophy gleaming on the mahogany desk. Jan watched Lotus, heavy with her coming litter, sleeping peacefully beside her sable daughter.

"I guess our dogs are like people," she said, looking affectionately at the two Shelties. "They're sometimes grouchy and quarrelsome, but they really love each other. Just look at those two, how glad they are to be together again."

At the approving tone of Jan's voice, Sissie wagged her tail happily.

There was no longer any doubt. She had earned her place. Sissie belonged, once and for all, at High Point.

10

A Well-Trained Dog

"I don't care if Sissie *does* have her Companion Dog title," Jan Dalton insisted, "if Sissie were *really* well-trained, she wouldn't keep upsetting the den wastebasket or sneaking out of the yard when someone leaves the gate open. And she wouldn't keep barking at the paperboy day after day."

Jan, complaining to Gil while she dusted trophies in the den, was really exasperated over this last grievance.

"Wouldn't you think the dogs would know the paperboy by now? He's been on our route since we moved here. I just don't understand."

"But Sissie obeys in all the really important ways," Gil defended the sable and white Sheltie, who dozed peacefully between his feet, her slender muzzle resting on his right shoe. Lotus stretched as usual underneath the old mahogany desk, not caring that Sissie was in trouble.

"Well, Sissie is *not* my idea of a well-trained Sheltie," Jan emphasized as she polished the marble on Sissie's huge High in Trial trophy won at the recent show.

This seemingly harmless argument was the beginning of the two most nerve-wracking weeks of Sissie's life. Determined to mold Sissie into a well-trained dog, Jan declared war on Sissie's mischief-making. She kept a folded newspaper handy and did not hesitate to punish Sissie with a loud thwack across the rump — which startled and humiliated Sissie rather than hurt her.

If Sissie pulled crumpled tissues out of the wastebasket — thwack!

If Sissie chewed the fringe on the den rug — thwack!

If Sissie barked at the paperboy — thwack!

Finally, Sissie learned that while in the house with Jan, her safest course was to curl up and sleep. She learned, too, that only her rawhide bone could be safely gnawed without Jan's brandishing the folded newspaper. Even Sissie's beautiful High in Trial trophy failed to shield her during Jan's crusade for good behavior. Playing was no fun anymore. So Sissie stopped playing and moped.

Jan was pleased with Sissie's "progress."

Gil didn't like the change is Sissie's behavior, but went along with Jan to keep peace. Sissie was doing so well in her obedience lessons, however, that Gil taught her to "drop on recall," that is, to drop in her tracks on command while she was at a distance from him. Sometimes he called to her to *down*! But he also trained Sissie to drop when he raised his hand over his head.

Sissie liked this new game, especially when Gil made a fuss over her. His praise and Jan's was all Sissie needed to be happy.

But although Sissie's manners in the house improved, she still barked furiously whenever the paperboy made his rounds. From the first thump of the paper on the neighbor's porch until the boy's bike

had long since disappeared, Sissie went wild. With unreasonable fury, she leaped against the fence and assailed Jan's ears with a cacophony of yips, barks, and ki-yiii's until Jan thwacked her on the rump with a folded newspaper and scolded harshly.

Ears down, humiliated and ashamed, Sissie would slink contritely to Jan for forgiveness. Jan forgave. But Sissie's rudeness toward the paperboy continued. Saddened because Jan never seemed pleased with her anymore, Sissie picked at her food. Her coat became dull. She was just not the same old Sissie. Even their neighbors, the Weigles, noticed the difference in Sissie.

"Have you been working her too hard?" pretty, blond Sue Weigle asked worriedly, scratching Sissie's belly while the Sheltie lolled blissfully belly-up.

"Could be," Gil admitted guiltily.

Gil shortened Sissie's training sessions, but nothing seemed to change her attitude toward the paperboy. The daily commotions continued.

One mellow Saturday afternoon after Labor Day, the peace was shattered by such fearsome yapping that a passerby would have thought that ten dogs lived at High Point. A whirling dervish of rust and white twisted to attack her enemy through the front door.

"Sissie!" Gil thundered. The anger in his voice brought Sissie to a contrite huddle at his feet.

"This has gone on long enough," he decreed. Then he went to the door and returned leading, or rather pulling, a freckled boy about thirteen years old. The boy had left his sack of papers outside.

When the paperboy entered the living room, Sissie stopped barking and calmly appraised the youngster, who froze with fear of being torn limb from limb.

"It's all right, Pete," Gil assured him. "If the dogs make friends with you, they won't bark so much when you deliver papers."

Sissie licked Pete's hand. Pete drew back warily.

"Yes, Sir, can I go now, Sir?" Pete asked, still leery of Sissie although she seemed friendly.

At last Pete was persuaded to extend his hand for Sissie to sniff. Sissie licked his fingers and wagged her tail. The introduction was complete.

"Now there'll be no more barking when you come, Pete," Jan assured the nervous boy. "Sissie seems to like you."

"I'm sure glad to know that," sighed Pete. "I always wondered how they'd act, especially the brown and white one, if there was no fence between them and me."

For the first time since Pete had entered the house, the corners of his mouth stopped twitching and relaxed into a smile. The Daltons smiled too, confident that Sissie's barking at the paperboy could now be controlled.

But they were wrong. The next morning, Sunday, Sissie aroused the household at seven o'clock when the thick Sunday paper was delivered. All the following week she continued to bark insanely whenever Pete approached.

"Sissie must be stupid," wailed Jan in despair. "That's the only possible explanation."

"But she learns everything else so quickly," Gil defended the sable and white Sheltie who now nuzzled his leg, begging for a rawhide toy to play with. "How could Sissie have won that beautiful trophy if she were stupid?"

"Maybe I'm expecting too much of Sissie," Jan mused. "After all, she's just a dog."

"Just a dog?" echoed Gil. "You always thought that dogs were very intelligent, Shelties especially."

"I don't know what I think now," Jan replied. "I still love Sissie, of course, but I don't have so much faith in her as I used to."

At mention of her name, Sissie ran to Jan and licked her hand. Sensing that Jan was displeased with her made Sissie miserable. Jan petted her, but without enthusiasm, and she didn't fool Sissie.

Monday was a pleasantly warm Indian summer day. Late in the afternoon, Gil relaxed in the backyard after teaching English to his high school students all day in a stuffy classroom. Only cicadas broke the silence at High Point as Gil sipped a cold soda and waited for the paper.

A distant thump transformed the lazy peace into turbulence, however, when Pete approached with the papers. Lotus stood up, barked dutifully, and flopped down into the cool grass. But Sissie, as furious as Gil had ever seen her, yipped shrilly with maniacal furor, leaping against the gate, growling and barking at Pete as though he were a thief or an intruder. Hot and angry, Gil threatened Sissie with a folded newspaper in his hand.

What he saw next stunned him. Pete, less afraid now that he had been face to face with Sissie and found her friendly, was *opening the gate* to bring the paper and collect payment for the week.

But as Pete opened the gate, a bronze and white rocket hurled against him, knocking him sprawling to the concrete walk.

"Sissie!" Gil shouted, horrified to see Sissie attacking the youngster.

Recovered from the initial shock, Pete got up and turned to run. Sissie pursued him, leaping up to tear and slash at newspapers — those terrible folded newspapers that he brought every day — those same folded newspapers that Jan used to spank and humiliate her with. Determined to destroy those awful papers, Sissie chased Pete down the driveway.

Gil ran after them, angry and sweating. If Pete had only stopped until Gil caught up, the incident would have ended, but Pete didn't stop. Sheer terror drove him to his bike. He kicked at Sissie, jumped on his bike, and pedaled down the road as fast as he could.

Just as Sissie sprang into the road after the boy, an enormous trailer truck thundered toward her. Pete maneuvered around the truck and disappeared. Sissie started after him.

"Sissie!" shouted Gil from the edge of the highway.

Sissie stopped and turned. If she continued across the road, the truck could not avoid hitting her. From the opposite direction a car now approached. Sissie stood confused in the middle of the road. All her instincts told her to chase her enemy — those awful papers. But her bond with Gil made her want to obey him.

Gil saw that Sissie's only chance for survival was for her to stay where she was. Otherwise, her graceful body would be tossed broken and bloody into the gutter like the countless unfortunate rabbits and squirrels and other wildlife. Not daring to call her to him lest the car hit her, Gil raised his hand high like a traffic policeman, the signal to "down." Speechless with tension, he waited for Sissie's reaction.

When Sissie saw Gil's signal, she dropped down and stayed, exactly as she had been trained to do.

The semitrailer thundered past in one lane, the Pontiac sedan whizzed by in the other. Sissie remained lying in the middle of the highway — safe.

At the first break in traffic, Gil called weakly, "Sissie *come*!"

Sissie bounded to Gil and was hugged and praised lavishly. Then she raced Gil to the house.

"I saw from the window," said Jan. "It was just the papers she was after, not Pete. Suddenly I realized that we've been punishing her with folded newspapers and Sissie didn't want Pete to bring any more. Isn't Sissie *smart?* And if she hadn't obeyed your signal to drop in her tracks...

If a tear trickled down Jan's cheek, Gil didn't see it because Sissie licked it away immediately.

"Sissie obeyed. When it *really mattered,* Sissie obeyed," Gil marveled.

With her loved idols so obviously pleased with her, Sissie wagged all over ecstatically.

A phone call to Pete's home verified that the boy, though upset by the harrowing chase, had arrived home safe. Gil suggested that it was wiser for Pete to collect at the front gate from now on and promised that Sissie would not chase him again.

It took several months before Sissie lost her suspicion of newspapers and became friendly with Pete. But never again was she punished with a folded newspaper.

And never again did Jan say that Sissie was stupid.

11

Gentleman Jim, the Saint, and the Double Zinger

That September Sissie's advanced training began in earnest. Gil enrolled her in obedience school, where dog owners were taught to train their own dogs. Along with a dozen other dogs of various breeds in Beginner's Open class, Sissie hopefully would develop into an Open obedience dog and earn the title of Companion Dog Excellent, or CDX. She already had mastered many of the advanced exercises — retrieving, retrieving over a high jump, dropping on command, and sitting or lying down for several minutes with Gil out of sight. But for Sissie to perform these tasks flawlessly amid the confusion and noise of a dog show, she needed to participate in a class with other dogs.

Before Sissie's education could proceed smoothly, both Sissie and Gil had two unexpected lessons to learn: trainer Gentleman Jim was no gentleman; and Sally the Saint bore no semblance to anything heavenly.

Sissie and Gil heard Trainer Jim several minutes before they actually met him. As they approached the knot of dogs and people who composed the Beginner's Open class, the authoritarian bluster of a drill sergeant boomed out of the group's center and crashed against their eardrums. And that was before the lessons even started.

The voice blustered from beneath a neat black moustache on a large, square-jawed face that fit a big man dressed western style in fringed suede jacket, white cowboy hat, and boots. Gentleman Jim was about to whip his scraggly band of recruits into shape.

Gil and Sissie took their place between a golden retriever named Whiskey, who whined incessantly, and a black Labrador retriever named Devil, who bristled with energy and couldn't sit still. A Saint Bernard named Sally strained her leviathan bulk against a thick leash held by a young woman. The other students — a Doberman, three German shepherds, a pug, and two poodles — seemed in awe of Jim and the newness of the situation.

Trainer Jim started the group out with a fast heeling exercise, and never had Sissie run so fast to keep up with Gil. "Forward, right turn, left turn, about turn" — Jim shot commands in quick succession. Unused to the fast pace, Sissie worked sloppily, annoyed by Whiskey's whining and Devil's panting. Above all, however, Sissie tried to stay as far away as possible from the mammoth Saint Bernard. Sally's massive head and lolling tongue frightened Sissie into heeling as close to Gil's leg as a shadow.

"Hold it! Hold it!" yelled Jim. "You guys are terrible! Worst Open class I've ever seen. Everybody wake up and wake up those dogs. You call that heeling? How did you turkeys ever manage to pass beginners' work? Watch your dogs, talk to 'em, and when they lag, *zing* 'em!"

"Do what?" asked Gil timidly, doubtful, even before he knew what it meant, of whether he wanted to "zing" Sissie.

"A zing is a good correction using the choke collar," Jim explained. "One good correction is worth a thousand words."

A choke collar was standard equipment for training a dog. But Gil always had kept the lead attached to the "dead" ring — which meant that the collar would not tighten up when jerked. Jim insisted that choke action be used for correction when needed.

Sissie's first "zinger" came when she lagged behind Gil on an about turn.

"Sissie, heel!" Gil commanded, jerking the lead. Sissie panicked as the choke collar tightened suddenly around her neck. Why was Gil punishing her? What had she done? She hurried to catch up with him. Then she heard "Good girl, Sissie," and after that she scrambled to glue herself to Gil's left leg.

"How do I zing a Saint Bernard?" asked the slim young woman, who was struggling to train the enormous dog. Sally seemed no more aware of the jerks on the collar than she would have been had a flea hopped onto her thick coat.

"With a lot more pep than you've been using, young lady," Jim boomed. The girl shrugged wearily and resorted to using both hands to strengthen her corrections. Sally just lowered her head stubbornly and continued to lag.

"Don't forget to praise your dogs when they're good," Jim shouted as handlers "zinged" away at their sloppily working students. "Praise immediately after each correction." Gil didn't need to be told to praise Sissie. He had been praising and encouraging her all along. He felt guilty about the "zingers" but saw that it was an effective training technique if properly used.

The most difficult exercise for Sissie was "figure eight." In this exercise, two people or "posts" stood about six feet apart while handler and dog heeled in a figure-eight pattern around them. Gil would start out slowly around the near turn, then speed up around the far post, lengthening his stride at the same time. Invariably, Sissie fell behind.

"You with the Sheltie!" Jim pointed to Gil. "You're six feet two or three inches tall, right? That dog is fifteen *inches* tall at the shoulder, right? Somehow you two have got to learn to walk together. Remember, you're not running for a bus."

But Gil's uneven stride continued to plague Sissie and cause her to lag.

"No use," Jim shook his head during one particularly frustrating training sesssion when Sissie lagged badly on "figure eight."

"Give her two zingers — one going into the far turn, another coming out of the turn. Try it. Forward."

Gil started out with his usual short stride, with Sissie glued to his left shoe. But try as Sissie would, when Gil swung his legs in extra long steps around the far post, she couldn't increase her stride fast enough to keep pace. So the "double zinger" became a miserable part of Sissie's lessons.

"Why isn't Sissie improving?" Gil complained to Jim after three sessions of "double zingers" and a still lagging Sissie.

"Look at her, looks like she's just been beaten," Gil groaned, miserable to think that he was breaking Sissie's spirit and causing her to hate working.

"I think that we can solve the problem next week," Jim said.

"How? If next week, why not now?"

"You'll see." Then Jim turned his attention to the problems of the other dogs. The black Labrador, Devil, would dash after his dumbbell with such exuberance that he would overrun it by several feet. Jim held a metal folding chair at the far side of the dumbbell after the handler had thrown it. Then, as Devil dashed by the dumbbell, unable to stop because of the momentum of his rush, Jim let the metal chair crash to the concrete floor. Devil braked, picked up the dumbbell, and raced back to his handler. At the next throw, Devil again dashed out crazily, but when he saw Jim standing there with the chair, he seized his dumbbell and hightailed it back to his handler, who praised him enormously. Devil wagged all over with a sense of accomplishment.

Whiskey, the golden retriever, was not so lucky. Every time that he whined, Jim handed a bottle of Tabasco sauce to the slim, blue-jeaned brunette who owned the handsome dog.

"A couple of drops down the hatch every time that he whines in class,' Jim ordered.

Gil winced. He hated Tabasco sauce and could imagine how a dog would react. He was right. Whiskey shook his head, lay his big yellow head between his paws, and gazed up at his mistress in horrified disbelief. But he stopped whining! And he did not whine again during class that day.

Sally, the sulky Saint, was a more serious problem. Not only did Sally work very slowly, which might be expected for such a heavy dog, but she kept eyeing her classmates, especially Sissie, as if they were good to eat.

"What worries me," Gil told Jan after training one Sunday, "is whether that girl, Hilda I think her name is, can hold that hulk of a dog if Sally should really take after another dog. Sally looks at Sissie as though she's a piece of liver."

"Well, I wouldn't want a dog that weighed more than I did," said Jan. "Let's hope that Sally doesn't eat Shelties for breakfast. Maybe she's not as mean as you think. Maybe she just wants to play."

"She hasn't exactly done anything bad yet, but there's a look in her eye. Frankly, the long 'sits' and 'downs' scare me. We go out of the building, you know, while Jim stays with the dogs. If anything happened, could Jim handle all those dogs by himself?"

"From what you've told me about him, he could. I think that next Sunday I'll come along and see for myself what goes on."

* * * *

The following Sunday was unusually cold for mid-October, even in Wisconsin. Already the ground sparkled with diamond chips of frost, and wind crocheted leaves into an amber and black afghan. All classes were held indoors now, and the short-haired dogs modeled brightly colored winter coats. Exhilarated by the crisp air, Sissie pranced to class beside Gil and Jan.

All the regulars were there: Whiskey, who was not whining; Devil, sitting calm and subdued beside his master; and Sally, sulking gloomily at her handler's feet. Jan recognized all the dogs from Gil's descriptions. When Jim entered clutching his customary cup of black coffee and cigarette and shivering in spite of his rust suede jacket, Jan identified him immediately.

Before class started, Jim greeted each dog by petting him and talking to him.

"Hi, Devil, old buddy, how are you today? Sissie, I see you brought both mommy and daddy today. Whiskey, do you still like Tabasco sauce with your dog biscuits?" And so on down the line. Each dog wagged its tail, sensing Jim's goodwill — every dog, that is, except Sally the Saint.

Sally lowered her head morosely. Jan looked admiringly at the great beast and wondered if Sally knew how powerful she was.

The delay in starting class made Gil fidget. Jim seemed to be stretching out his greeting procedure. A sudden commotion at the door explained the delay, however. In trooped a television camera crew from Channel 12, which was going to spotlight the training school as part of a special feature.

As cameras clicked away, Jim directed the class to heel in unison, making frequent left and right turns.

"Not bad, group," Jim commended them. "Now I'm going to have only one dog and handler perform the 'figure eight' for the cameras. Mr. Dalton, bring Sissie out."

Gil couldn't believe it. Sissie was one of the worst in the class. Why would Jim want to embarrass them? As he and Sissie performed the "figure eight," with Sissie lagging as usual, Gil's ears burned red with humiliation.

The last two exercises were "long sit" and "long down," with handlers out of sight. All handlers lined up and told their dogs to stay, then left the building with Jim watching over the eleven dogs.

The camera rolled steadily, shifting from dog to dog.

Suddenly Lena, a nervous Doberman, got up and edged toward the door. Jim grabbed her choke collar quickly and slipped the leash that Lena's handler had left behind her dog. This disturbance seemed to annoy Sally. The Saint Bernard lowered her head like an angry bull and stared belligerently at the dogs on either side of her and at the cameramen. Whiskey began to whine. Sissie, three dogs down the line from Sally, looked around nervously for Gil.

Without further warning, a brown and white volcano erupted toward Sissie. Jan screamed as Sally hurtled toward the sable and white Sheltie. With lightning reflexes, Sissie leaped away as though she were flying over a hurdle, but Sally, moving with surprising speed for her bulk, snatched a mouthful of hair from the "frill" on

Sissie's left hind leg before the Sheltie could scramble out of reach of the gargantuan teeth.

After that first onslaught, Sissie raced to Jan and scooted under her chair just as Sally hurled her mountainous bulk toward them.

Sally never reached her goal. A huge, weathered hand seized the charging Saint by the collar, and Jim's thick, powerful body wrestled Sally down as though she were a calf. His right hand on the collar administered a giant zinger, while his left arm levered the Saint into submission.

"Get the others," Jim yelled to Jan, who for the first time realized that the other dogs were either standing about in confusion or racing toward the door.

As quickly as she could, Jan grabbed up the leashes left behind each dog and fastened leashes to collars, looping each leash around a chair leg. She worked without thinking whether any of the dogs would resent her, and in a minute or two she had all the dogs anchored except Sissie, who kept to her cave underneath the chair while Jim straddled the winded Saint and talked soothingly to calm the giant dog.

Gil never forgot the scene that greeted him on his return, nor did he forget the horrible questions that haunted him. What if Sissie

hadn't been so fast? What if Jim hadn't been so strong? What if Jan hadn't acted so quickly and fearlessly in rounding up the dogs?

"Sissie would have been mush," he said. "That Saint would have chewed her up and spit her out."

"Don't think about it," warned Jan. "The danger's over. Sissie had her speed to protect her. And Jim knew what to do."

Gil shook Jim's big mitt of a hand and thanked him.

"It won't happen again," Jim reassured him. "At least not with Sally. We'll keep her tied while she's on a long sit or down from now on. By the way, don't forget to watch the ten o'clock news tonight on Channel 12 — I want you to see that film."

Jim turned to the camera crew, who were shaken by the unexpected violence in their assignment.

"We really gave you guys a show, didn't we? God, what a morning! Will someone please get me another cup of black coffee?"

* * * *

At ten that night, Jan brought two mugs of steaming coffee and a plate of oatmeal cookies into the den and turned on the television. World news came first, then local happenings, and finally the week's feature, starring Sissie and her classmates. As Gil watched himself and Sissie performing the "figure eight," he leaned forward and became more and more excited.

"Jan, look at that! Do you see what I did? I started out taking short steps, and then all of a sudden I swung my right leg forward and took a giant step around the far post. Sissie couldn't possibly speed up quickly enough to keep up with me. It's me, Jan, it's my fault! It's not Sissie's fault at all!"

Sensing his excitement, Sissie jumped into Gil's lap and nuzzled his face. Gil laughed and hugged her and rumpled her silky ears.

"Sissie, I know what to do now to improve our 'figure eights.' All I have to do is learn to pace properly, and you'll keep up with me, won't you, Girl?" The wriggling of Sissie's tail told him that she would certainly try her best.

"Now you know why Jim picked you and Sissie to demonstrate that exercise."

"My respect for that man grows every week," said Gil. "We're lucky, Sissie and I, to have such a good trainer. Just think, Sissie, no more double zingers, at least not on 'figure eight.' "

And although Sissie didn't know what Gil said, she showed her wholehearted approval by thumping her tail happily against his shoe and nibbling daintily on the oatmeal cookie that he sneaked to her when Jan wasn't looking.

12

A Matter of Relevance

With "figure eight" under control, Sissie made rapid progress in obedience school. So skilled did she become in performing her lessons, in fact, that Gil started giving her even more advanced lessons on his own. Picking out an article with Gil's scent on it was one of Sissie's new lessons.

"What's that?" asked the Daltons' neighbor, Sue Weigle, cynically, looking up from her coffee mug to watch Gil teach Sissie to discriminate scents one Saturday morning in the fall. As Gil worked, Jan and Sue sipped coffee and dunked donuts on the patio.

"It's a metal dumbbell," Gil explained. "The idea is to hold it in my hand until my scent is on it, then to place it among similar but unscented articles. It's up to Sissie to pick out the one I've touched. She should be able to do the same with any object that can hold a scent."

"But what for? I don't see any practical purpose for it," Sue Weigle said, brushing back her blond bangs and looking amused. Sue liked Sissie for the self-confidence that the sable Sheltie had given to her crippled son, Mark. Sue had even testified in Sissie's behalf in court, but she still didn't always see the sense of obedience training.

"It lacks — relevance!" was her verdict, as she watched Sissie select the correct dumbbell and return it to Gil.

"Well, relevant or not, someday Sissie will be ready for Utility work, which is like college for dogs. And scent discrimination is one of the required exercises."

After the lesson, Gil praised Sissie extravagantly. Then the happy sable and white Sheltie streaked onto the patio for more praise. Jan scratched behind Sissie's ears, but Sue Weigle managed only a polite pat on the head. Sue was here to go antique hunting with Jan, and she was eager to get started.

It was a gorgeous October day. In Wisconsin, even a hazy fall day has charm. But clear, brisk days, when the sky is cornflower blue — such days are gems to be hoarded in the memory as a squirrel stores nuts for the winter's famine. Today was such a day, a fantasy to be reconstructed from memory during a blizzard and used as a beacon of hope that the world would once again be warm and fruitful.

"If you're driving out in the country, why not take Sissie? It might be a good idea to have a dog along in case of car trouble," Gil suggested as the two women prepared to leave.

"Sissie may be small, but she barks loudly," he coaxed.

Sue Weigle made a face. Reluctantly she agreed but hoped that Sissie wouldn't get dog hair on the upholstery of her car.

When Jan opened the hatchback door and beckoned to Sissie, the overjoyed Sheltie leaped in, delighted at the invitation. She sensed that this was not a trip to the veterinarian or to the hated boarding kennel, and she welcomed a chance to go along with Jan.

The women had made their plans. They would drive north about seventy miles to a little community of artists, look at paintings and antiques, then have lunch and browse until they were tired. The weather was cool enough so that they wouldn't have to worry about leaving Sissie in the car while they shopped.

The drive itself was a treat. The sun illuminated the sumac trees to lantern-glow orange. Chalk-white birch trees crowned with sequins of gold shimmered against the sapphire sky. Like spilled port wine, scarlet leaves splashed across the landscape to complete a picture of rich harvest. The land that had produced food, shade, and havens for young animals during the summer was celebrating in jewels and party clothes before resting for the winter in a dark gown and white robe.

Sissie enjoyed the ride immensely, eagerly sniffing the brisk air redolent of wonderful country things like partridge and rabbit.

When Sue and Jan left her alone while they went shopping, Sissie got a little restless, but soon she was ready for a nap in the warm sunshine. She curled up on the red shag rug that Jan had brought and fell asleep.

When the women returned with their purchases, Sissie greeted them happily. Jan took Sissie for a short walk. Then it was lunchtime, and once again Sissie was left alone in the car. She was really bored and fidgety now, but this time she found some interesting packages to investigate.

The juicy hamburger that Jan brought back made the wait worthwhile. And Sissie thoroughly enjoyed her walk with Jan on the restaurant grounds before they got in the car to begin the drive home.

"I couldn't look at another vase," laughed Sue, starting the car, "or examine another saltbox to see if it really was 200 years old."

"Did you see that 'Early American' oil lamp that had 'Made in Hong Kong' stamped on the bottom?" asked Jan, and both women laughed at their shrewdness in spotting fake antiques.

"Caveat emptor," said Jan. "Let the buyer beware."

"Oh?" exclaimed Sue. "I always thought that meant 'beware of the dog.'"

"Want to stop anywhere else?" asked Jan in high spirits.

"Let's go straight home," Sue said. "I can hardly wait to show Howard the Early American snuffbox I found. That really is a treasure."

"Does Howard use snuff?" The idea seemed curious to Jan.

"Heavens, no. Cigars are bad enough."

"Then why'd you buy a snuffbox?"

"Because it's rare and valuable, and, well, it's an heirloom." Something she saw in the rearview mirror caused Sue to pull over to the side of the road and stop.

"Why are we stopping in the middle of nowhere? What's wrong?"

"My snuff box!" Sue nearly choked as she turned to retrieve the neatly wrapped package that she had left on the rear deck of the hatchback with Sissie. One corner of the package had been gnawed open. Sue ripped off the rest of the paper and ribbon to reveal her snuffbox intact with one slightly scratched corner.

"It's ruined! My antique's ruined! And it's Sissie's fault!"

Jan felt terrible. She held the snuffbox up to Sissie and said "shame" several times. Sissie knew that Jan was unhappy with her and lay down with her head between her paws. But it had turned out to be such a boring day — even the few toys that she had found had turned out to be forbidden.

"I'll have it restored for you, don't worry," Jan promised, and Sue calmed down somewhat.

"Oh look!" Sue shrieked, pointing across the road to a stand of golden aspen so beautiful that she momentarily forgot the snuffbox.

The grove of aspen was a study of yellows from antique gold to ochre, daffodil to chartreuse; leaves continually floated down like feathers burst from a gigantic pillow.

"I've got to have some of those leaves for my new vase and for Mark to take to school for Halloween," Sue insisted. "If I can't have my snuffbox, at least I can take home some leaves. No argument. Let's go."

Sissie was overjoyed at the chance to crunch through the leaves that gave off an intriguing, nutlike odor. The sunshine, though still warm, was waning now, and a chilly breeze shook leaves down faster than before.

Unaware of the fading sunlight, Sue and Jan gathered several clusters of foliage. But a beautiful spray of leaves always lay just a yard beyond, and after half an hour of garnering, they lost sight of the road. Sissie was having a really good time.

"Time to head for home," warned Jan, looking up. "Dusk falls quickly out here."

The hike back to the car took only ten minutes, but a strange look came over Sue's face as she fumbled in her purse for her keys.

"They were right next to my wallet, I'm sure," she muttered, while Jan waited patiently for her friend to start the car.

"Or did I slip them into my pocket when we stopped?" She searched her pockets, examined the floor on the driver's side, then finally emptied her purse on the car seat.

"They're gone! It's impossible, but my car keys are gone!" She was nearly crying. The light was fading fast now as dusk came on.

"I must have dropped them," Sue moaned. "How could I be so careless? But that's what must have happened. I guess we'll just have to wait in the car with the doors locked and the flashers on and hope that the county police patrol this highway," Sue groaned, realizing the odds against finding her keys in all those leaves.

"I'd like to try one thing first," said Jan. "Give me one of your gloves."

"I don't have any gloves with me," Sue replied, puzzled.

"Your wallet, then, give it to me."

"What is this, a holdup?" But Sue did as her friend asked, grasping at any hope.

Jan let Sissie sniff the wallet. Then she gave a command.

"Sissie, find it!" and she pointed in the direction that their leaf gathering had taken them.

Sissie raced off nose deep in dusky bronze leaves, sniffing along the path that still bore their scent. But what was she supposed to find? Confused, she returned to Jan after a few minutes, wagging her tail but with her head lowered sheepishly. She knew that she had failed.

Jan petted her, then took her own house keys out of her purse and handed them to Sue.

"Here, hold these a while," she directed, and Sue pressed the keys between her nervously sweating palms until Jan was satisfied that they bore Sue's scent.

Then Jan let Sissie smell the keys.

"Sissie, find it," she again commanded.

Once more Sissie raced off and soon became invisible as her shaded sable coat blended into the darkening ground cover. Now Sissie had a clearer idea of what she was looking for. She sought something with a metallic scent, something hard. Following the trail that they had taken earlier, she poked her long muzzle frequently into the musky leaves.

The women waited nervously beside the car. It was nearly dark, and this was not a well-traveled road.

"Sissie, come!" Jan shouted, then waited anxiously for the Sheltie's return. Being in a wilderness alone at night was not reassuring.

Then they heard rustling and saw flashes of white ruff as Sissie galloped up to Jan and thrust her muzzle into Jan's outstretched hands, depositing in them Sue Weigle's car keys.

Later, after a phone call to Howard Weigle explaining her lateness, Sue joined the Daltons for a supper of scrambled eggs, toast, and coffee. After supper, Gil examined the snuffbox that Sissie had scratched. Tired from the nerve-wracking events of the day, Sissie rested at his feet.

"We'll have it restored," Gil promised. "But seriously, Sue, in today's world, is a snuffbox really relevant?"

"Don't rub it in," complained their guest, pushing back her blond bangs and peering up mischievously. "We've had a rough day."

"I wouldn't do that," Gil protested. "It's just that there's some interesting lettering underneath the snuffbox where Sissie chewed through the veneer. Some Revolutionary War code, no doubt."

"Let me see that." Sue scrutinized the "code" for a long time.

"Now why," asked Gil, "would the American colonists have coded this snuffbox 'Taiwan'?"

A very quiet moment followed.

"Sometimes it's difficult to know the real thing when you see it," Gil pronounced with mock solemnity.

Then Sue Weigle began to giggle, and Jan joined in. Before long, three very foolish-looking people rocked helpless with laughter while a russet and white Sheltie ran from one to the other, happy to be sharing the fun. Sue picked up Sissie and hugged her, not caring whether or not a few dog hairs clung to her navy blue cashmere sweater.

"Sissie, you're a very *relevant* Sheltie."

Sissie wagged her tail in appreciation of the compliment but what really delighted her was the square of buttered toast that Sue Weigle slipped her when Gil and Jan were not looking.

13

The Ice Princess

"I say wait until Sissie has her CDX," said Gil, looking up from the pile of papers that he was trying to correct.

"But Sissie's young; now's the time to breed her," Jan argued. "Besides, why should Lotus have all the burden of raising puppies?"

"Sissie's making good progress at obedience school. I say let's see how she does in the fall Achievement Trial. If she works well, let's enter her in some shows before she gets involved with motherhood."

Jan relented, and they bred Lotus to a fine Champion Sheltie that had won many Best of Breed awards.

"Maybe we'll keep a male puppy," Gil said with a sideways glance at Jan.

"Oh, Gil, you know we agreed not to keep a male — we're too small a kennel yet to have a stud dog."

"Maybe, but I'm outnumbered here by girls. I'd just like to even things up a bit. And a scrappy male puppy would be fun for all of us, especially Sissie."

Sissie wagged her tail as if ready to play with the new puppies. Lotus, unconcerned about the coming youngsters, slept under the mahogany desk.

* * * *

In the middle of October, the Daltons took Sissie to a local "fun match" to show her in conformation — that is, for beauty, soundness, and movement. Jan had agreed to groom and show Sissie for this show since no obedience work was involved.

They arrived early and enjoyed a breakfast of donuts and hot coffee while waiting for Sissie's turn. Jan had bathed Sissie the night before, so a good brushing and spraying with coat dressing was all that Sissie needed to make her coat glisten like polished copper.

As Jan picked up her armband at ringside, however, the ring steward informed her that someone had reported to the judge that Sissie was over the allowed height of sixteen inches at the shoulder.

"Ridiculous!" snorted Jan, but Sissie had to suffer the humiliation of being measured with a U-shaped metal wicket set over her back like a giant hairpin. Nothing in her training had prepared her for this shameful episode. Sissie was measured at fifteen and one-half inches, well within the standard height.

"Who called for the measurement?" Jan asked Gil, but Gil knew as little as she did, and the judge did not tell them. Only three Shelties waited to be judged in Sissie's class. But the catalogue listed a fourth.

When finally the latecomer paraded into the ring to join the other dogs in her class, whispers of disbelief echoed around ringside. Jan nearly dropped Sissie's leash.

"That's her, that's Snowball!" someone said.

"She's — she's white! A white Sheltie! Is that allowed? I never saw a white Sheltie."

Indeed, Happydale The Ice Princess — "Snowball," as she was called — was white as a snowball molded of fresh, virgin snow. Scarcely anyone there had ever seen a white Sheltie, and yet there stood Snowball, white as a Samoyed but with light blue eyes and a few gray and tan body spots of the color seen in blue merle Shelties and collies. The most striking feature was her completely white head with very small, pink-rimmed eyes.

"Is she an albino?" Jan asked.

"No, a double-merle white," Gil told her. "An albino would have pink eyes and a pink nose. Snowball's eyes are blue, and her nose is black."

"She *is* pretty, but would any judge dare to put her up? I thought that white wasn't allowed."

"White isn't a disqualification," Gil said, "but a judge is supposed to penalize a white Sheltie so severely that it probably would not be able to win."

The crowd buzzed as they tried to absorb the phenomenon of the white Sheltie.

Inside the ring, Jan set Sissie up in her best pose. But she still couldn't take her eyes off Snowball. Mrs. Erickson of Happydale Kennels wore a royal blue dress against which the marshmallow white Sheltie stood out in stunning contrast.

The judge, looking very English in his country tweeds and salt-and-pepper moustache, examined each dog carefully but kept coming back to Snowball.

When he asked the handlers to move their dogs around in a circle, Sissie stretched out her strong young legs and glided around the ring without so much as a ripple of her smooth back. Snowball lacked Sissie's flowing gait.

A blue merle with a very long coat looked gorgeous when she stood still but waddled when she walked. A young tri-color, obviously in need of more training and experience, balked and pulled so hard on her lead that she almost choked.

The judge placed Sissie and Snowball side by side and scrutinized the two beautiful dogs. Sissie looked taller than Snowball because of her long, arched neck; Snowball was stockier and lacked Sissie's gracefulness. Then the judge stepped back and thoughtfully studied the four Shelties. The outstanding two presented a contrast — one white and very unusual; the other fox red and elegant.

Finally, he pointed to Sissie as winner of the class and placed Snowball fourth behind the acceptably colored dogs. Mrs. Erickson stalked out of the ring angrily, not even waiting for her ribbon.

"Too bad," commented the judge, "she is a lovely animal, but the breed standard requires that whites be penalized."

"Talk about sore losers!" muttered Gil, until Sissie interrupted him by jumping into his lap at ringside.

That day Sissie went on to win Best Sheltie in Match, a very nice win for a young dog. Mrs. Erickson was not among those who congratulated Jan and Gil.

"Why was Mrs. Erickson so angry?" Jan wanted to know after they got home. "And who asked the judge to have Sissie measured?"

"What it all means," Gil told her, "is that Sissie has an enemy, someone who wants to see her disqualified from competition. As to who it is, your guess is as good as mine."

"I simply have no idea." Jan was baffled. "The idea of Sissie's having an enemy is outrageous."

"Not to someone who's out to defeat her in competition," Gil repeated.

"Well, I can't solve that mystery now, but I have another. Something bothers me about Snowball. Did you see how she watched Mrs. Erickson and nothing else? Never took her eyes off Mrs. Erickson or the liver that she was holding? Even when it started to rain and there was that loud pounding on the roof, Snowball looked as though she were carved from vanilla ice."

"Maybe that's why she's named The Ice Princess — because she's so calm and imperturbable," Gil guessed.

"I have a feeling that we haven't seen the last of Snowball," predicted Jan, bending down to scratch behind Sissie's ears.

And so that day ended without any of their questions having been answered.

* * * *

The following Sunday, Sissie's obedience school held its Fall Achievement Trial to measure the progress of its students. Gil would soon know if Sissie was ready for serious Obedience Trial competition.

"Why Mrs. Erickson," he heard Jan say on their way to the ring. "I didn't know that Snowball was a student here. I've never seen you here before."

"Oh yes, we're old members," was the icy reply. "Snowball dropped out to have puppies, and now we're getting back into training." Mrs. Erickson, vivid in a bright red pantsuit, stooped to pat Snowball, whose eyes never left her handler.

"Well, here we go. Come on, Snowball." Mrs. Erickson gave Snowball the signal to heel and started toward the ring.

Fascinated by the white Sheltie, Jan and Gil watched Snowball turn in a beautiful performance, made even more remarkable by the fact that Mrs. Erickson never spoke to her dog but worked her entirely by hand signals.

"There's your answer to why Snowball watched Mrs. Erickson so closely, Jan. Snowball's trained to respond to hand signals."

"But why does Mrs. Erickson work her *only* on signals?"

"Why not? Sissie responds to hand signals, too. I just don't use them often in the ring. There's too much chance of her glancing away for a second and missing a signal or, at an outdoor show, of sun getting in her eyes."

"But Snowball does it and never misses a signal!" Jan continued to be amazed and baffled by the white Sheltie and perhaps even a little jealous because the dog's obedience work was as dazzling as her appearance.

Then it was Sissie's turn to show what she could do. Sissie started out with a smooth heeling performance, sticking to Gil's left heel like a shadow. "Figure eight" was equally good now that Gil had learned to measure his stride and not speed up suddenly. Retrieving looked easy when Sissie flew after her dumbbell and returned it eagerly to Gil, first on the "flat," with no obstacles, then over a two-foot-high solid hurdle. Similarly, the four-foot broad jump presented no problems for Sissie.

"Good work, Sissie," Trainer Jim was there to congratulate them as they left the ring. "You're on your way, Sissie, ready for the big shows. You'll be a Companion Dog Excellent by spring." Jim's big mitt of a hand stroked Sissie's muzzle affectionately.

During the long sit, Sissie sat next to Snowball. After the handlers had left the building, they milled around nervously, waiting for the three minutes to pass so that they could hurry back to their dogs. Some smoked, some talked or just stood tensely and hoped that their dogs were behaving. The obedience school's spacious

grounds were hushed as autumn lingered between acts waiting for a Wisconsin winter to take its cue.

Suddenly, the calm was shattered by several loud explosions. The ring steward ran out of the building yelling, "Hurry, everyone, back to your dogs!"

Inside, the handlers found a chaotic scene. Only one dog remained sitting where it had been told to stay. All the other dogs had stood up and moved as bullets peppered the roof. Some now cowered under chairs; others, Sissie among them, wandered aimlessly in confusion.

"Hunters, poaching on our grounds, hunting for pheasant," the ring steward explained. "Stray bullets hit the roof. Everybody stay inside until we clear this up."

And while several of the men investigated the disturbance and routed the poachers, the handlers returned to their dogs and prepared to repeat the exercise if the judge was willing to give them a second chance.

Only Snowball had remained sitting, an ivory figurine seemingly oblivious to the commotion around her. Snowball did not have to repeat the long sit. And Snowball was awarded first prize in the class.

Threats of prosecution frightened off the poachers before they could fire any more shots. Fortunately, no serious damage had been done to the roof, and most important, no one had been hurt.

"Some Achievement Trial," Jim commented after normalcy had returned. "Only one dog was well enough trained to stay through all that ruckus. Excuse me, I need some hot coffee."

"That's the answer," said Jan enigmatically after Jim had gone.

"What answer to what question?" asked Gil.

"The question of what's been bothering me about Snowball. She's deaf. That's why nothing bothers her. She's completely unaware of any noise. And that explains why Mrs. Erickson works her entirely by hand signals."

"But deafness is a disqualification, both in obedience and conformation."

"Right. The American Kennel Club doesn't permit a deaf dog to be shown."

"So what do we do about it? Snowball is winning illegally as far as the American Kennel Club is concerned. Do we report her?"

"Why should we be the ones to tattle? Remember, Sissie was just beaten by Snowball. Doesn't it look like we're poor sports if we report her?"

"Whoever told the judge last week that Sissie was oversized wasn't a very good sport either," Gil said bitterly.

"Yes, but are you sure that it was Mrs. Erickson? And even if it was, should we stoop to her level? Isn't there a better way to make our point?"

Jan and Gil were puzzled by the dilemma.

As the Achievement Trial came to a conclusion, it became clear that no dog had equaled Snowball's nearly flawless performance, and it was to the white Sheltie that the High in Trial trophy was awarded. As Mrs. Erickson and Snowball left the ring highlighted by the flashbulbs of picture-snapping admirers, Gil approached them.

"Congratulations on Snowball's beautiful trophy, Mrs. Erickson. She worked extremely well," he said. "By the way, may I have a word with you?"

"I'm in a hurry to get home. Snowball's hungry."

"We're in a hurry, too, but I just wanted to ask you if you were the one who called for Sissie to be measured at that match last week."

The point-blank question astonished Mrs. Erickson.

"Why, well, Sissie *is* a large Sheltie — much larger than Snowball."

"Sissie looks taller than Snowball because she has a longer neck, but she's still well under the height limit. And she is totally sound."

"I'm sure she is," Mrs. Erickson muttered impatiently, edging away from Gil.

"I just wanted you to know," Gil told her quietly, "that I would not want to be the one to report an unsound dog — a deaf dog, for instance — to the American Kennel Club without absolute proof. I would try to obtain proof, however, if I thought that such a dog was being misrepresented to the public and to dog show judges."

"I see," said Mrs. Erickson dryly, not quite so impatient to leave now. "And what should the person you suspect of showing such an 'unsound' dog do about it?"

"He has to do what's best for the dog and for the reputation of Shelties."

"Good-bye, Mr. Dalton, good luck with that oversized Sheltie of yours. No matter what the judge said, I know that she's too big."

Gil stooped down and clasped Snowball's snowy muzzle between his hands, the way Sissie liked.

"You're a beauty," he said to the lovely unhearing Sheltie, who looked at him with her gentle blue eyes and sweet expression, "and you're *almost* perfect."

Snowball wagged her white plume of a tail as she bounced off beside Mrs. Erickson.

"Sometimes the dogs are nicer than their people," was Jan's comment after Gil recounted his conversation with Mrs. Erickson. Sissie jumped up against him and wagged her tail, impatient to go home.

"Good Girl, Sissie, you did well today. And you did win a nice second-place trophy."

Snowball was not seen at any more dog shows, either conformation or obedience, but her High in Trial award at the obedience school's Achievement Trial went unchallenged. No one ever disputed the white Sheltie's right to the honor that she had won.

14

A Boy and His Dog

At the beginning of December, Lotus whelped a small litter of three puppies — two sable boys and a tricolor girl.

"Just look at these little guys — solid as rocks." Gil hefted the plump, ratlike puppies, still moist and warm from their journey into the world.

"This one's ugly, though," Gil added, wrinkling his nose and pointing to one male puppy whose head was predominantly white. "Too much white; he looks like a cow."

"Oh, he's not so bad, and he may grow into those markings." Jan defended the puppy that now scrambled against Lotus's side looking for the source of warm milk.

"Just remember," said Jan firmly, "no stud dog at High Point yet. Remember our agreement. And no buts."

"But — " Gil trailed off helplessly. Jan was right. They had agreed to keep only females for awhile. Money to show a stud dog was still scarce, and it would be wiser to wait.

Although Lotus growled at Sissie when her daughter approached the new family, Sissie was ecstatic over the new arrivals and could hardly wait to play with them. Several times a day, she crept up to the whelping box and tried to get a closer look at the wriggling babies snuggled close to Lotus. But Lotus's growling reminded her of nature's rule — a mother has sole dominion over her babies while they are suckling.

The weeks passed quickly as one of the worst winters on record gripped Wisconsin. Prolonged periods of Arctic cold punctuated by foot-deep snowfalls compounded the Midwest's fuel shortage. The president urged that thermostats be lowered to conserve fuel.

The Daltons set their thermostat at sixty-two during the day and sixty at night. Those temperatures were fine for the dogs indoors, but whenever Sissie and Lotus went outdoors, the frigid cold numbed their paws, and ice balls became wedged between their toes. Even a romp with Jan or Gil was no fun for the dogs in such weather. Cold was the adversary of people and animals alike.

But in spite of the cold, the puppies grew strong and lively, and soon Lotus and Jan had their paws and hands full: cleaning puppies, feeding puppies, chasing puppies, and playing with puppies. Sissie helped with the playing.

The little tricolor girl was promised to a friend who had long wanted a Sheltie, and one male puppy was reserved for Mark Weigle, whose overprotective parents never seemed to get around to buying a puppy for the handicapped child. Even though Mark still used crutches, the Daltons thought him well able to care for and train a dog. And surely the loving relationship would be good for him.

"Are you sure that Sue Weigle will agree to take the puppy?" Gil asked skeptically. "I'd hate to give Mark a dog, have him get all excited about it, then have Sue bring it back complaining about dog hair or the puppy's being too much trouble to housebreak."

"I'll check with her first before I say anything to Mark," Jan promised. "But I want Mark to have the puppy with the sable face. He's got a nice, outgoing personality."

"What about this boy?" Gil asked, holding up the handsome red sable puppy with the wide white blaze that swept up his short muzzle over his head and blended into a wide white collar.

"You were right. Too much white on his face," said Jan. "I don't like him."

"But what a friendly little guy he is," Gil pleaded like a child coaxing his mother to buy him a puppy.

"Remember, no buts."

"But this *is* a fine puppy in spite of the white blaze. We couldn't do much better if we went shopping for a dog."

"Maybe not, Gil, but he's for sale, and I've placed an ad in next Sunday's paper for him."

"Shouldn't we hold him for awhile to see how he develops?"

"And give you a chance to become attached to him? No!"

* * * *

The ad was answered by a thin, nervous lady with a pale boy about twelve years old. The child was fascinated by the white-faced puppy, which the Daltons had named Rocky.

"Let's get him, Mom, let's get him now," he pleaded, hugging Rocky roughly. Gil was a little worried over the child's lack of gentleness but figured that boys and dogs have a way of working things out.

"We're moving up north next week," explained the mother, Mrs. Whitaker, "and there may not be a nice Sheltie for Joey in that area. So we thought we'd get the puppy now."

Gil didn't like the sound of this. A puppy had enough difficulty adjusting to a new home without having to readjust to new surroundings after only a few days. But Mrs. Whitaker and Joey liked Rocky and agreed to pay the asking price. Jan took the money and packed Rocky a bag of food and his favorite toys.

Gil handed the puppy reluctantly to the eager boy.

After the Whitakers had gone, Gil stared straight ahead, pretending to watch television, while Sissie nuzzled his leg, trying to cheer him up. Jan felt terrible when she saw how the loss of Rocky affected Gil.

"I'm sorry, Honey, we should have kept him. I didn't realize he meant that much to you."

"Well, it's done now. I'm really being silly. As long as the little fellow has a good home, I'll get over missing him. Then one day Sissie will have puppies, and she'll let me have one of them, won't you Sissie?"

At the returning hint of playfulness in Gil's voice, Sissie leaped into his lap. But Gil didn't feel playful and remained unhappy over the loss of the white-faced puppy.

A few days later, the tricolor girl, Pixie, went to her new home. The Daltons were satisfied that she would be a much loved and pampered pet.

The Weigles seemed pleased at the Daltons' offer of a puppy for Mark. On the pretext of "just going over to see the puppy," Mark's parents took Mark next door and let him play with Rocky's brother, a bouncy sable.

"Want to take him home, Mark?" Gil asked the happy boy.

"Would I! He'd be my buddy forever," Mark said wistfully, as though already envisioning the fun that Buddy and he would have together.

"He's yours, Mark for you from all of us — Jan, me, Sissie, and Lotus. We can't think of anyone better to raise and love him."

"Oh, Mr. Dalton!" Mark could hardly speak, only hugged the squirming, playful puppy closer.

"I'll name him Buddy. And he'll really be my closest buddy."

"A boy and his dog," said Gil, "make a great combination."

"How about a girl and her dog?" asked Jan mischievously.

"Same thing — a winning team. Like me and Sissie, right, Girl?" Sissie was having a wonderful time with all her favorite people so happy. Licking faces and wagging her tail, she ran from one to the other. When Sissie brushed against Sue Weigle, however, Gil noticed Sue grow tense and make a face as she brushed imaginary dog hairs from her navy blue pantsuit. Gil sensed trouble but hoped that the irresistible Buddy would win her heart as he had Mark's.

"What do you think?" Gil asked Jan after the Weigles had departed in a flurry of last-minute questions and instructions.

"So far, so good, give them a chance. They're new dog owners, and like most people, they'll adapt. Besides, we're close by to help if there are problems."

So the puppies were gone, and Sissie moped around the house looking for her lively playmates. She missed the rough tumbles with the energetic babies.

But no one missed the puppies more than Gil missed Rocky. And he worried about the puppy with the wide blaze.

"Let's call to see how he is," Jan suggested, sensing Gil's anxiety over the puppy.

"They just moved, remember? We haven't got their number."

"That's right. But I can write to the old address and the letter will be forwarded. I'll ask Mrs. Whitaker to call collect or to write us about Rocky."

Jan wrote, and while the weather worsened, they waited for a response. On subzero days, Sissie and Lotus fretted restlessly in the house. Only for short periods of time could they stand the cold that combined with bitter winds to produce a deadly windchill.

The Saturday after Valentine's Day, a phone call came from Mrs. Whitaker.

"How do you like your new home?" Jan asked politely. "And how is little Rocky?"

"We love our new home and Rocky is fine, but I didn't think that he was going to be quite so shy."

"Shy?" asked Jan, alarmed. "Rocky was one of the friendliest puppies I've ever seen."

"Well, he's under the kitchen table now, just shaking. That's all he ever does — hide under the furniture and shake."

"Are you gentle and patient with him?' Jan asked, rather impatiently.

"Well, yes, but of course he has to be punished when he's naughty in the house. And all this trembling upsets my husband. He likes a livelier dog."

Jan got the drift. The Whitakers probably expected Rocky to behave like an adult dog — sensible, obedient, and clean. Anyone who became angry with a three-month-old puppy shouldn't own one, Jan thought.

"We'll be up today to get him and give you a full refund," Jan offered resolutely. "I think that's best for all of us."

The Whitakers had moved 200 miles north, and the unstable February sky threatened to dump heavy snow on the winter-weary Wisconsin landscape.

"Let's go," said Gil firmly. "Ignore the weather. Let's get Rocky." And soon they were on their way, with Sue Weigle promising to feed Sissie and Lotus. When they were two thirds of the way there, the snow started, and from then on they crawled northward over increasingly slippery highways. Snow tires helped, but high winds made every mile hazardous.

"Shouldn't we stop at a motel and wait out the storm?" Jan advised, weary and a little frightened.

"I'd rather not," Gil persevered. "If Rocky's being mistreated, I want to rescue him as soon as possible."

But he finally did yield to Jan's judgement, and they sought refuge in a motel for the night. After a light supper of hamburgers and coffee, they called the Whitakers to check on how close they were. They had come within ten miles of their destination, yet common sense kept them from trying to complete their mission during a blizzard.

By morning the worst of the storm was over; only high winds remained to cause drifting and send the windchill factor plummeting. After toast and coffee, the Daltons hurried to the Whitakers' to get Rocky.

Mrs. Whitaker met them at the door, even more nervous and fidgety than they remembered her. Joey stood behind her, sulking. Just as Mrs. Whitaker had described, Rocky huddled under the kitchen table, retreating further into his cave when anyone approached.

Gil got down on his hands and knees and softly called the puppy's name over and over. For a minute, Rocky ignored Gil and continued shivering. Then memory lighted his little dark eyes, and the white-faced puppy zoomed out from his cave with the fury of sudden recognition. It was a joyous reunion. Gil and Rocky rolled on the floor until Gil realized how undignified he was acting and picked up the puppy.

"Let's go home, little fellow," he said, while Jan paid Mrs. Whitaker.

Joey still hung back, a sour look of disappointment on his face. Finally he spoke.

"It was a dumb puppy. Dad didn't like it. Dad likes German shepherds and Dobermans, all those big dogs. Dad didn't like Rocky at all."

"Maybe your next puppy will work out better, Joey," Jan said gently. "Maybe when you're a little older, you'll learn how to take better care of a puppy." Jan could see that although the boy was truly unhappy about losing Rocky, he was unable to cope with his father's disapproval.

The Daltons left the unhappy home as quickly as possible.

"I loved seeing you with Rocky again," Jan said as they headed for home. "Just a boy and his dog. Like Mark Weigle and Buddy. Looks like Sissie has a rival."

"No way! Sissie's so special that she could never have a rival in my feelings," Gil affirmed. "But there's room at High Point for Rocky, too." Rocky just curled up on the seat between Jan and Gil and fell asleep.

Late Sunday afternoon they arrived home. The Weigles, who were outside shoveling snow, came running over to find out how their neighbors had fared driving through the snowstorm.

Sissie and Lotus, ecstatic at Rocky's homecoming, raced around the yard with the puppy out of sheer joy. Gone was the quaking, fearful Rocky that had to be coaxed out from under a table.

The situation next door, the Daltons soon found out, was not so happy.

"Mark's starting to sneeze at night," Sue Weigle complained to Jan. "Of course, Mark insists on Buddy sleeping in his bedroom. That will have to stop."

Almost every day Mark brought Buddy to visit the Daltons. Lotus, Sissie, Rocky, and Buddy galloped pell-mell around the yard, occasionally tackling each other and generally having a good time. But Mark's mood did not always match Buddy's exuberance.

"A puppy is a lot of trouble for Mom," he confided to Jan. "While I'm at school, she has to take Buddy out a lot and wait for him to be a good puppy. And at night Buddy doesn't always use newspaper like he's supposed to, and Mom gets mad."

"You should confine Buddy to a small area at night, Mark, like in a cage, or even barricade him in the kitchen, where there's a tile floor. He'll soon learn to wait until morning."

"Another thing," Mark continued. "Dad says that I breathe heavy at night since we got Buddy. They're afraid I'm getting asthma."

That night Jan and Gil discussed the Weigle situation.

"They'll never let Mark keep Buddy," Gil prophesied. "We might as well start looking for a new home for him."

He was right. A week later, Sue Weigle called to say that Mark was becoming asthmatic from the puppy and that the doctor had decreed definitely no dogs or cats for a couple of years. Buddy was returned to High Point and advertised for sale. A young couple claimed him at first sight of the lively sable and white youngster.

Mark continued to come over to play with Rocky and to put Sissie through her obedience routine. One afternoon Gil put his arms around the brooding child and hugged him.

"Guess I'm just lucky, Mark. I've got Sissie and a puppy, too, but you'll have to wait for your dog. One day Sissie will have puppies, and I promise you your pick of the litter if you've outgrown your asthma."

"Gee, do you think I'll get over this asthma?" Mark asked longingly, wanting to believe Gil.

"Meanwhile, you're welcome to play with Rocky and Sissie whenever you want to."

"Thanks, Mr. Dalton," Mark replied, a little more cheerful at the thought of someday getting one of Sissie's puppies.

"Oh, and Mark — " Gil called after the limping boy.

"Yes?"

"My mother wouldn't let me have a dog, either. My sister had all kinds of allergies. So make sure that you marry a girl who loves animals and has no allergies."

Mark laughed and patted Sissie, who escorted him to the gate, careful not to jump against the unsteady boy.

Once again Jan reminded Gil of their pact not to raise a male dog at High Point yet.

"Don't get too attached to Rocky, Gil. You know that we have to be objective about our dogs if we want to have top-quality Shelties."

But when Rocky bounced into his lap, Gil forgot to be objective. He had a hunch about the youngster: maybe the white-faced puppy would grow into the wide white blaze and turn out to be a Champion. And Sissie loved the puppy, too. In the meantime, while Rocky was growing up, they could enjoy him; there was no need to sell him immediately.

It was too bad, Gil thought, that Joey Whitaker and Mark Weigle would have to postpone the wonderful experience of owning a dog. His own boyhood was long past, but no one watching Gil Dalton sprawled on the den floor with Rocky jumping on his chest and Sissie playfully nipping at his shoes would argue that the boy in Gil had finally found his dog.

15

The Good Sport

All during that miserable winter, Gil Dalton worked with Sissie in the basement on her jumping and retrieving, preparing her for the three Obedience Trials that she must pass to earn her Companion Dog Excellent title.

Sissie disliked having lessons in the basement, where gloomy shadows startled her and concrete walls limited her freedom. But doing anything with Gil or Jan was fun, so Sissie paid close attention to whatever Gil wanted her to do. Soon she was close to perfection in performing her obedience exercises. Gil was delighted.

One morning at the end of February, Gil surprised Jan at breakfast.

"I sent in two entries for Sissie in Open class," he announced. "I think that she's ready to try for the CDX title."

"Are you sure that she's ready?"

"Yes. I'm afraid she'll get bored practicing the same exercises over and over. I want to enter her in shows while she's still enthusiastic."

For the next two weeks Gil worked with Sissie twice a day, keeping a strict, no-nonsense tone during lessons. Sissie knew that he was serious and tried extra hard to please. She loved her jumping and retrieving so much that lesson time was almost like play to her.

The show was well attended. Crowds filled the aisles, making passage difficult. Children eating hot dogs and adults drinking coffee sat so close to ringside that crumbs and cigarette ashes dribbled into the obedience rings, distracting the dogs. A juicy hot dog waved by an excited youngster was enough to tempt even the best-trained Sheltie.

Sissie disliked such crowded conditions and laid back her ears to show her unhappiness. The sensitive Sheltie would much rather have stayed home retrieving for Gil or Mark in the basement.

While waiting for Sissie's turn in the ring, Gil saw a young woman in a light green pantsuit practice throwing a dumbbell for her Sheltie to retrieve. The Sheltie, a lovely tricolor, gleaming jet black with white and tan markings, waved her plumed tail happily as she retrieved the object.

Suddenly, the tricolor Sheltie cried out in pain, and the happy tail drooped between her legs. Sissie looked up at the source of the outcry. The woman had seized the Sheltie by the ears and was jerking the unfortunate dog in front of her with the dumbbell in its mouth.

Gil ran over to the woman, who had not relinquished her hold on the Sheltie's sensitive ears and whose face had gone blotchy red with anger.

"Hey, what's the matter? Why are you hurting that dog?" Gil demanded to know.

"Darn dog won't come in straight," she replied. "Tessie knows better than that."

"But why hurt the dog? She won't learn anything from rough treatment. Besides, dogs aren't supposed to be trained on show grounds. That's an American Kennel Club rule."

"Butt out, Mister, mind your own business," the young woman snapped rudely, brushing her long, reddish brown hair away from her face. "You don't see me training my dog, and I don't see you training yours, OK? I'm willing to be a good sport about this."

"No, that's not OK as long as you continue to mistreat your dog."

Even though the redhead let go of the Sheltie's ears, the dog, Tessie, continued to whine softly.

Gil decided to report the incident to the show superintendent, but just as he started to hunt for the superintendent's office, he heard Sissie's number called over the loudspeaker and went directly to the obedience ring.

With Sissie heeling close beside him, he took a deep breath and stepped into the ring. The judge, a stocky, middle-aged woman with a businesslike look in her blue eyes, measured Sissie to check the height that she would have to jump, then asked Gil if he had any questions. He did not.

"Forward," said the judge, and the exercises were underway. Sissie heeled well, although Gil thought that she lagged on the about-turn. She did the drop on recall exercise perfectly, just as she had the day that she had chased the paperboy. She performed the retrieving exercises smoothly and accurately, both on the "flat" and over the high jump. Only the broad jump remained.

Just as Gil was ready to give Sissie the command to jump, he heard a squeal and turned his head. The redhead with the tricolor Sheltie was waiting outside the ring and must have hurt her dog to make it cry out. Gil seethed with anger, but at the moment he knew that he must concentrate on Sissie's work.

"Send your dog," ordered the judge, and Gil gave the command "Sissie, over!" Sissie did her part beautifully and received a nice round of applause.

Gil saw that the red-haired woman in the green pantsuit had not applauded. Why should she, he thought, when she was competing against Sissie for trophies?

"Not everyone's a good sport, Sissie," he told his happy Sheltie, who was enjoying having her ears scratched while savoring a smidgen of hot dog donated by an admiring little girl. Only long sits and downs remained to complete Sissie's work.

Next it was the the tricolor Sheltie's turn to compete. From the way the black, white, and tan Sheltie looked up at her handler, Gil could see that the little dog wanted to please. But the redhead obviously would settle for nothing less than perfection — a heavy burden to place on a dog, even a Sheltie.

"I don't mind Sissie's losing to a good working dog," Gil told Jan, "It's just that I hate to think of that woman mistreating that fine little dog and getting rewarded for it by winning blue ribbons and trophies."

"Maybe she isn't really that bad," Jan tried to calm him. "She may love the dog very much, but maybe dog shows make her tense and irritable. You must admit that showing in obedience isn't the most soothing hobby in the world."

"Then she has no business training and showing fine, sensitive dogs," Gil asserted. "There is no excuse for cruelty."

Silently, the Daltons watched Tessie, the tricolor Sheltie, complete a flawless figure eight. The red-haired woman didn't even praise her dog for the good work.

The next exercise was drop on recall. The woman heeled Tessie to the opposite end of the ring; then, at the judge's signal, she called Tessie. Tessie trotted obediently toward her handler but dropped down at the halfway point before the command to drop was given. Anticipating a command was an automatic disqualification.

The redhead ran toward Tessie, who crouched in wild-eyed terror, and, contrary to American Kennel Club rules that prohibit correcting a dog in the obedience ring, she grabbed the poor Shelite's ears and jerked the dog toward her. Tessie screamed in pain.

But not for long. The judge, a big woman herself, seized the handler's arm, forcing her to release Tessie.

"Shameful!" the judge shouted. "You're disqualified. Leave the ring immediately. And don't let me see you hurting that dog."

The red-haired woman handler complained of injustice to everyone outside the ring who would listen. Most turned away in disgust.

"Wait till I get you home," she told the cringing, terror-stricken Tessie. "I'll beat you into a decent obedience dog yet."

"Will you sell her?" Gil asked as he took out his checkbook.

"Are you serious? This is a valuable show dog."

"Will you take $100 for her right now? That's all I can afford today, but if that's not enough, maybe we can work something out."

"Take her for the hundred. I'm so disgusted I don't want to look at her again."

Gil wrote the check quickly before she could change her mind.

"Please send me her registration papers right away," he said.

"Sure, as soon as I get home."

Gil doubted that he would ever get Tessie's papers, but he didn't care. The Sheltie's welfare was his only concern.

He didn't have much time to get acquainted with Tessie before the steward called the Open A dogs into the ring for the long sit. While Gil took Sissie into the ring, Jan held Tessie in her lap and soothed the frightened little dog with the sad dark eyes.

After the long sit and long down exercises were completed, Jan, Gil, and the two Shelties waited at ringside until the qualifying dogs were announced. Sure enough, Sissie's number was called. This meant that she had qualified — that is, scored at least 170 points out of a possible 200 and had passed every exercise.

After all the qualifying dogs had lined up in the ring, the judge prepared to make the top awards.

"In first place," the judge announced, "with a score of 196 out of a possible 200, is Sheltie number 72."

Gil glanced at his armband as though he could not believe that he and Sissie were the winning team. His fingers trembled as he accepted the blue rosette and handsome bronzetone trophy that the judge handed him. With a different handler, he thought, Tessie might have won this class. The little tricolor had been denied her moment of glory. It was Sissie's day to excel; Tessie's time would come later.

Outside the ring he hugged Sissie and showed her the handsome trophy topped by a winged victory figure, which, of course, meant nothing to Sissie except that this shining object evidently caused her people to be quite pleased with her. Sissie preferred to sniff Tessie, who shyly sniffed back, and the two were friends.

"Let's go home, Sissie. Come on, Tessie," called Jan, gathering up her things. Tessie, her shyness rapidly fading, trotted eagerly beside Sissie toward the exit. It had been an eventful day.

"Well, Sissie, you've got the first leg of your CDX title and a trophy besides. That's a terrific start."

"Don't you mean that Sissie won five legs?" queried Jan.

"How so?"

"One leg of her obedience title and Tessie's four legs. First, Rocky comes back home, and now we have Tessie. Do you realize that in spite of all our good intentions, High Point Kennels is having a population explosion?"

"That's all right," Gil laughed. "Today was a good day — good for Sissie and good for Tessie. Everything will work out, you'll see."

And together they all raced to the car, full of the high spirit that winning brings.

16

Of Tough Judges, Fashion, and the Green-eyed Monster

Tessie was such a sweet, eager-to-please Sheltie that at first Jan and Gil wanted to keep her. Sissie and Rocky liked her, too, and Tessie even tolerated Rocky's rough tackles as he bullied dogs and people into playing with him.

Only Lotus resented the newcomer. With menacing growls and snarls that raised her lips quivering over ivory fangs, she warned Tessie to keep her distance. The newcomer showed respect for the old dog.

"Lotus is only protecting her position as leader of the pack," Gil observed. "Dogs are pack animals, and someone has to be in charge. In this household, it's Lotus."

"But Tessie's such a quiet, sweet Sheltie. How could Lotus be so jealous?" Jan was puzzled and disturbed by Lotus's hostility toward the newcomer.

Lotus's stubborn resentment of Tessie continued to disrupt the harmony of High Point.

"If we sell Tessie, it must be to a very good, loving home," said Jan, "the kind of home we'd want for any of our puppies." Jan was becoming resigned to parting with Tessie. "I must be sure that she won't be mistreated again."

"I agree," Gil responded. "And I think that we should try to find her a home where she'll be the only dog. That way she'll be the center of attention."

The following Saturday night, the Daltons entertained some friends — a colleague of Gil's at the high school where he taught. When the teacher and his wife, who was expecting their first baby, saw Tessie's dark, searching, almond-shaped eyes and felt her moist nose nuzzling their hands, they felt the wonderful vibrations of knowing that they had found Their Dog. Never mind that Tessie was three years old, was slightly cow-hocked, and had no papers — she was Their Dog, and they were Her People, and the delight of Dave and Gloria Silverman lighted up their faces. Tessie would have a good home. The Silvermans chattered excitedly about Tessie as they thrashed the Daltons at bridge.

"That's the last time I invite Dave and Gloria to play bridge," Gil grumbled after their guests had left with Tessie. "They're too good for us."

"Good, maybe we'll learn something from them." Jan sighed. "I miss Tessie already. She was so eager to please and so dependent on kindness."

"She'll have a first-rate home with the Silvermans," Gil assured her. "I have a gut feeling about that. By the way, there just happens to be three little Shelties around here that may not always be eager to please, but they are equally dependent on kindness. Oh, and Jan, is there any of that onion dip left? I'm starved."

And three wet noses and three pink tongues reminded Jan that she wouldn't be lonesome.

* * * *

Sissie had little time to rest on the glory of her win. On the second try for a leg of her Companion Dog Excellent title, she had the bad luck to run up against the toughest judge in the Midwest, or at least this was the reputation of the slim, blond, young woman who recently had begun a career as an Obedience Trial judge.

Gil and Jan didn't hear the gossip about Bettina Gilman until after they had mailed the entry, and then it was too late to withdraw without losing the entry fee.

"We goofed," Gil concluded, stretching out on the den couch to take a break from correcting papers. "The word is that Tina Gilman is looking for scalps. She shaves the fine points thinner than deli ham and deducts the maximum for every little mistake."

"Isn't that what an Obedience Trial is all about?" Jan defended Tina Gilman. "The judge is supposed to visualize a perfect performance and deduct points from any work less than perfect."

"Well, if Sissie works well, I want her to get the score that she deserves. And I don't want any women's libber of a judge to get even with me for being a man by penalizing my dog's performance."

"Oh? A little edgy because so many good dog show judges are women? Shame on you, Gil, for being a male chauvinist you-know-what."

"Well, I don't even know Bettina Gilman. Sissie will probably do just fine. I even bought a new pair of slacks to wear to the show. My old lucky jeans are so faded and worn, I'm beginning to feel embarrassed. Give the old ones away."

Jan left for a few minutes and returned with two mugs of hot coffee and a plate of cookies.

"I suppose the fact that Bettina Gilman happens to be young, female, and blond has nothing to do with the new wardrobe?" Jan retorted, pushing her own hank of tawny hair back from her face.

"I wouldn't call one new pair of jeans a wardrobe. I thought that you were all for women judges. Say, do I detect a note of jealousy?"

"Me? Jealous? Of course not!" But Jan had heard that Bettina Gilman was strikingly beautiful.

Just then Sissie rolled onto her back and kicked her hind legs in an invitation for someone to scratch her belly. Jan obliged. Then Rocky charged pell-mell into Jan's lap in a fit of jealousy, so Jan scratched two bellies at once. A nibble of oatmeal cookie made everyone feel better, however.

"It looks like I'm not the only one subject to jealousy," she said.

"Rocky's a pest sometimes," Gil complained. "He could use some obedience training about now. Why don't you tackle it, Jan? Why don't you train Rocky at the obedience school while I'm working with Sissie?"

"Well, I guess I can try," Jan agreed.

"Rocky will love the attention, and the exercise will be good for you. You always say that you don't get enough exercise."

"Now just a minute! Are you implying that my figure needs improvement?" Jan patted the seat of her size eight jeans.

"I can't win," moaned Gil. "I promise to keep my mouth shut for the rest of the evening. Except when I'm eating cookies."

* * * *

The following Sunday morning, Sissie and Rocky jumped into the back seat of the station wagon and went to school together. Although Sissie loved her playmate, she became annoyed when the white-faced puppy tried to shove her off the back seat, forcing her to do a balancing act to keep from being dumped onto the floor.

At school Rocky continued to be a pest. Upset to see Rocky receive all of Jan's attention, Sissie kept twisting around to watch them, much to Gil's annoyance.

"Sissie! Pay attention!" he ordered, giving Sissie a zinger, which she hadn't needed for a long time.

"Sissie's lagging badly and heeling wide!" Trainer Jim scolded. "Come on, Sissie, sharpen up!"

But much as Gil tried, he couldn't get Sissie's undivided attention when Rocky and Jan were nearby.

"Behave yourself, Sissie. I'm even wearing my new jeans for you so you'll get used to them before the next show. And Gil brushed dog hair from the new pants, which were cut fashionably longer and wider than his old jeans.

"Sissie's jealous — that's the trouble," Jan analyzed. "She's heeling wide and turning around to watch Rocky and is not paying attention at all. Sissie'll never be a CDX at this rate."

It was true that Sissie was heeling wider than usual as though trying to avoid Gil. And she lagged on the about turns and on "figure eight." Also, when she retrieved the dumbbell, she sat too far away from Gil, a sure point loser. Sissie sensed that Gil was displeased with her because he didn't call her a good dog or scratch behind her ears. It seemed to Sissie that Rocky was the one getting petted and fussed over.

As a result of this friction, at Sissie's next Obedience Trial, the last weekend in March, Rocky was left at home. Gil wore his new jeans and a new light blue shirt topped by a faded denim jacket.

"Very sharp," Jan approved. "For me, Sissie, or Bettina Gilman?"

"Sissie's not the only one influenced by the green-eyed monster," Gil kidded her, fastening his armband in place.

"I've got grounds. Take a look at Ms. Gilman, your judge."

New judge Bettina Gilman was ready to start the Open A class. Her long, blond hair swung down over her shoulders. Dressed in a dark blue pantsuit that emphasized her lithe young figure, she scrutinized every detail involved with her judging assignment. Carefully, she straightened the mats and measured the jumps, not leaving any detail to the ring stewards alone. Gil glanced appreciatively at the lovely young woman who obviously intended to do a thorough job of judging.

The class started and so did Bettina Gilman's pencil. Constantly and rapidly, she checked mistakes of each dog on her judge's score sheet.

"Look at Bettina's pencil fly," commented one trainer at ringside. "Tina's well on her way to becoming the toughest judge in the Midwest."

"Doesn't miss a thing," said another handler.

Gil noticed that the glamorous judge spoke for a short time to each handler after his dog had performed the exercises.

"What's she saying?" asked Jan.

"Probably pointing out mistakes," Gil guessed.

Then it was Sissie's turn to perform, and Gil was gazing into Tina Gilman's cool hazel eyes as she asked the usual "Any questions?" and "Are you ready?"

"Yes," said Gil.

"Forward," commanded Tina Gilman, pencil poised, and the routine was underway. Sissie heeled without lagging, but she worked too wide, not hugging Gil's left leg as she used to do. And when Gil swung around on the about turn, Sissie made a wide arc around him. As Sissie worked, Ms. Gilman's pencil kept busy marking mistakes. Gil felt that he and Sissie were turning in a miserable performance.

But on the recall, retrieving, and jumping, Sissie's work improved greatly. She ran out readily for her dumbbell and returned to sit squarely in front of Gil. She performed equally as well on the retrieve over the hurdle. And she sailed over the broad jump for a perfect score on that exercise. Gil felt better as he left the ring.

After all the dogs had completed the exercises, Jan, Gil, and the other handlers waited at ringside to learn who had qualified and who had won trophies.

The loudspeaker blared Sissie's number and that of a miniature schnauzer who had worked very well. The two dogs were tied and would compete in a runoff to determine the winner.

"Oh, no!" groaned Gil. "Sissie's never been in a runoff before. What do we do?"

"The judge will tell you," a friend said.

Gil's hand shook as he clutched Sissie's leash and lined up beside the schnauzer's calm handler, a young woman who looked as though winning runoffs were no new experience for her. Gil noticed that although the girl wore her dark hair in the fashionable short wedge style, she wore old-fashioned pipestem jeans.

"Ready? Forward!" ordered Tina Gilman, and Gil and the schnauzer's handler said "heel" and started off briskly with their dogs. Sissie heeled fairly close to Gil, though she lagged just a little behind him. The schnauzer shadowed his handler's pant leg as though part of a welded unit.

"Halt!" said Tina Gilman. Gil halted. The schnauzer's handler halted. The schnauzer stopped instantaneously with his owner. Sissie also stopped simultaneously, but then, as Gil's pant leg swung toward her from the momentum of the sudden halt, she edged away slightly to avoid the flap of denim from the flared jeans.

Tina Gilman pointed to the schnauzer as winner. Sissie would have to settle for second place.

"At least Sissie earned the second leg of her CDX," Gil showed off Sissie's second-place trophy, a beautiful brass cup mounted on a walnut base. "I am a little disappointed, though."

"I think that Tina Gilman wants a word with you," Jan nudged him, and Gil turned to see the pretty blond judge smiling and beckoning him back into the ring.

"Uh-oh, what now?"

Back in the ring, Tina Gilman's searching hazel eyes turned warm, and she smiled as she talked.

"You know, you have a really fine working dog there," she complimented Sissie.

"Thank you, but her heeling was not as good as usual today."

"That's what I wanted to talk to you about. Why spoil a dog's good performance by wearing wide-cut pants that flap in the dog's face, especially on halts and turns?"

"What?" Gil was amazed that he had not thought of such a simple solution to Sissie's poor heeling.

"In plain words, your slacks are swinging into your dog's face. They look great, but not for training and showing dogs."

"Thank you, thanks for telling me," Gil sputtered, embarrassed as though he had just been told that a zipper was open. But he was grateful to Tina Gilman for her forthrightness. Tina extended her hand, and Gil shook it warmly.

"Hey, what were you two so chummy about in there? Shaking hands like old friends."

"She's quite a gal. And a good judge, too."

"I thought that you were disappointed about Sissie's losing the runoff. Well, never mind, what did she say to you?"

"Oh, nothing very important. By the way, Jan, did you throw away my old jeans like I told you to?"

"Your what? Why bother about that now?"

"Well, did you?"

"Of course not. They're still good for gardening and washing the car and all sorts of chores."

"Including dog training."

"What? No more new outfits for dog shows?"

"No more flared jeans flapping in Sissie's face. Poor Sissie. I've been scolding her for something that isn't even her fault."

But Sissie wasn't unhappy at all. Just the opposite — with Jan and Gil giving her all their attention and slipping her morsels of pretzel and donut, she couldn't have been happier. And without that sassy Rocky interfering, Sissie had her loved people all to herself. For the moment at least, all the monsters in her life, including green-eyed ones, had been banished.

17

The Dark Hours

The days that Mark Weigle came over to put Sissie through her obedience routine were special days for Sissie. She loved Mark and had learned to be extra careful not to jump against him too forcefully as she had once done, sending the crippled boy sprawling. Again and again, Mark sent Sissie to fetch her dumbbell until Jan had to warn him that, much as Sissie liked to work and play, she did get tired.

Sometimes Mark and Sissie and Rocky played roughhouse games in the basement. Tug-of-war with an old sock or a glove was Sissie's favorite.

One blustery Saturday morning in early April, Jan loaded her washing machine and went upstairs to groom the dogs, a regular weekend chore. While she was trimming Sissie's nails, she heard a "kapokita-kapokita" from below that boded no good. She found sudsy water flooding the basement. By noon a serviceman had repaired the leak, but a slippery residue remained to be scoured from the basement floor — a tedious hands-and-knees job.

"It never rains, it pours," Jan complained to Gil after detailing the drudgery of her day.

"What about 'misery loves company'?" Gil countered. "Look at this pile of tests that I have to correct tonight. That's the worst part of being a teacher. How come I always have more papers to correct than you do?"

"Because I'm so efficient," Jan taunted.

After supper, while Gil worked on his tests, Rocky teased Sissie into chasing him around the house. Later, Sissie stretched out at Gil's feet and, when Gil reached down to scratch behind her ears, she wagged her tail happily. Jan read a novel and forget about the irritations of the day.

On Sunday morning, High Point had visitors: Dave and Gloria Silverman brought Tessie for a visit. All Tessie's shyness was gone; in a loving home she had blossomed into a bright-eyed, vivacious Sheltie, eager to work and play.

"Dave's taking Tessie to obedience school," said Gloria. "I wanted to train her myself, but I won't be much good at bending down until after the baby's here." Gloria laughed warmly as she demonstrated her difficulty in bending down to pet Tessie. Tessie cooperated by jumping up to kiss Gloria's plump cheek.

While the Daltons and the Silvermans had coffee, Sissie, Tessie, and Rocky raced around the yard in a joyful reunion. Lotus, though remaining aloof from the fun, did not seem hostile to Tessie now.

After their guests had gone, Gil helped Jan wash dishes.

"That's one story with a happy ending," he said.

"Really. Aren't they wonderful together? Tessie fits perfectly with their personalities and life-style."

"Remember, Tessie will have to share the spotlight with a baby soon."

"I wouldn't worry about that. Tessie will love the baby."

* * * *

On Monday Mark Weigle limped over after school, and all the dogs welcomed him. After a snack with Jan of chocolate chip cookies and milk, Mark hobbled down the basement stairs, Sissie close behind him, keeping out of the way of Mark's unsteady feet and crutch. The jumps were set up in the usual places, but Mark failed to notice that the rubber mats that provided a safe grip for Sissie as she jumped and landed were missing.

First Mark threw Sissie's dumbbell several times for her. Then he tossed her dumbbell over the high jump.

"Sissie, get it!" he commanded, and Sissie flew over the hurdle to retrieve her dumbbell.

She did not return with it. Instead of landing on her rubber nonskid mat, she slipped on the still soapy, slick floor and twisted her right hind leg. The pain made her forget the dumbbell. She quivered with bewilderment at why her legs suddenly could barely support her.

"Bad Sissie!" Mark yelled at her. "Get it!"

But when Sissie started to move toward the dumbbell, her hind legs collapsed beneath her, and she lay on the basement floor panting with shock.

Mark seized Sissie's collar and pulled her to her feet angrily. Then he recognized the pain in her pleading eyes.

"Mrs. Dalton, come quick! Sissie's hurt!" he shouted. Jan ran down the stairs to find Mark sitting on the basement floor cradling Sissie's head.

"The mats! I forgot to replace the mats!" Jan screamed, and, pierced with guilt, carried Sissie upstairs to examine her leg. Rocky and Lotus ran to see what the commotion was about. Gil was just getting home from a teachers' meeting.

"Sissie can't stand," Jan yelled at him in panic. "Her leg must be broken."

"She can stand," Gil said after examining the hurt leg, "but she can't walk. Get your coat."

The veterinarian diagnosed the injury as a torn ligament, a serious injury.

"Can you operate? Will she get well? Will Sissie ever jump again?" Jan's fears tumbled out in the form of questions.

"I could operate," said Dr. Stein, "but I think that we should wait and see how nature fares. Sometimes scar tissue forming around the tear strengthens the ligament. Right now there's no way of knowing how severe the injury is."

"It's my fault. I forgot the mats." Jan burst into tears.

"There's a good chance for complete recovery, Mrs. Dalton," Dr. Stein consoled her. "Wait and see. Keep Sissie quiet and don't let her exert herself. Carry her in and out of the house if necessary. Don't let her climb steps."

On the way home, Gil comforted Jan with the slim hope that Dr. Stein had offered. While they talked, Sissie slumped despondent on the back seat, her hind leg burning like fire and her body refusing to cooperate with what she wanted it to do. The pill that Dr. Stein had given her was making her drowsy. She lay quiet and closed her eyes.

"What if Sissie can never jump again," Jan complained. "She'll never be a Companion Dog Excellent."

"She will be to us. She'll still be our Sissie."

Jan felt ashamed because Gil was right. Nothing was important except Sissie's recovery. An obedience award was, after all, just a scrap of paper.

"Do you realize that in spite of all her pain, Sissie hasn't even whimpered?" Jan asked, aware for the first time of the sable Sheltie's courage.

At home, the Daltons kept Sissie quiet and away from the playful Rocky. This meant isolating her in the den. Several times a day Jan carried Sissie outside because the patient could not climb up or down even one step — her hindquarters were nearly powerless. Sissie could barely walk.

* * * *

Wisconsin springs are notoriously late. They arrive in carefully measured stages. First, in late February, the sun melts the snow's surface, but plunging temperatures glaze the runoff at night, transforming sidewalks to ice rinks. March reduces the snow piles, but at least one blizzard bends the backs of the junipers. Early April promises spring but cannot be trusted. Not until late April can Wisconsin people and animals sun themselves in the new season. And the fragrance of lilacs waits for May.

Throughout that chilly, wet April, Sissie lived with pain and loneliness. Medication soothed her pain, but nothing consoled her for the isolation that she endured. No lessons. No walks. No tug-of-war with an old glove. No mock battles with Rocky. No retrieving for Mark. Only Lotus, who slept much of the time lately, kept Sissie company in the den.

In the evenings, Sissie lay at Gil's feet while he corrected papers. Often Lotus would desert her favorite spot under the mahogany desk to lie beside her daughter while spring rains whipped High Point. The two Shelties rested and waited.

By the end of April, Sissie was walking better but still could not get up or down the back stoop unaided.

"She's improving. Let's postpone surgery indefinitely," Dr. Stein said hopefully but without promising miracles.

"I think that you can stop the medication," Dr. Stein added. "Sissie doesn't seem to be in much pain anymore."

That was very good news. At least Sissie was not suffering.

But just as Sissie seemed to be getting better, a new problem developed at High Point. Lotus lost her appetite and vomited repeatedly. Gil and Jan wrapped her in a blanket and drove her to the animal hospital, where, seriously ill with an infection, she underwent surgery. The Daltons returned home alone with tear-filled eyes.

And then Sissie was really lonely during the day while Jan and Gil were teaching. She missed her mother and couldn't understand why Rocky wasn't allowed to play with her. No matter how much the eager puppy whined and scratched at the den door, the door remained closed. Mark Weigle still visited several times a week, but life for Sissie was a shadow of what it had been. Her coat thinned, and her eyes grew dull.

After a few days, Lotus returned home, weak and scarcely able to walk, but Dr. Stein said that she would be fine. Now High Point had two invalids.

On the first day of May, after winds had driven away the clouds and left a dazzling blue sky, Sissie stepped gingerly off the back stoop unaided and felt warm sunshine penetrate and soothe her stiff leg. She listened to the birds chatter, smelled the waxy pollen of tulips, and felt stronger than she had in a long time.

Spring had finally come to Wisconsin.

But Sissie had lost her sparkle and her health.

18

No Place to Go But Up

The arrival of spring meant that the plagues of cold and snow were replaced by plagues of rain and mud. As frozen ground thawed, mud oozed everywhere, breaking up street surfaces, cracking sidewalks like miniature earthquakes, and coating with slime every foot and paw that ventured outdoors.

Snow shovels at High Point were replaced by buckets of water and piles of rough towels to cleanse paws belonging to Sissie, Lotus, and Rocky. After each outing, each paw had to be dipped in the bucket of warm water and toweled dry — a process often accompanied by much wriggling and splashing, especially on Rocky's part. The white walls in the back hallway became polka-dotted with brown spots, and the hall floor daily resembled a delta.

"I could plant tomato seedlings in the silt," Jan complained as she set to once again with mop and pail. "And just look at Sissie!"

The offending Sissie wagged her mud-streaked tail, adding stripes to the brown dots on the walls. This time Jan dunked Sissie's entire tail and fluffed it dry with a towel.

The Silverman's baby, a girl, arrived the second week of May, and Jan enjoyed shopping for tiny overalls and a fluffy yellow sweater for the baby. Tessie was thriving, Dave Silverman said, and was really part of the family now. Dave invited the Daltons to visit them in a few weeks when things settled back to normal.

But not even the sight of tulips sprouting through the thick black mat of last fall's leaves really cheered Jan Dalton. High Point Kennels was not prospering. Her hope that Lotus would have several more litters had been ended by the spaying operation that had saved Lotus's life. Jan had envisioned Sissie bringing home honors in the obedience ring and possibly even earning a Championship — these hopes also had evaporated. Even Rocky was failing to live up to his earlier promise. One of the white-faced puppy's ears hung so low during his teething period that Jan had just about given up hope that the fault could be corrected.

Still another problem developed. One Saturday morning, Jan received a call from Sue Weigle.

"It's about Mark. Can I come over and talk?"

"Is Mark all right? I mean, he's not sick, is he?" Jan asked with genuine concern. She dearly loved the courageous boy.

"I'll tell you the problem when I see you."

The call resulted in an all-morning coffee session during which Sue Weigle told a story of how Mark felt responsible for Sissie's accident. He felt that he should have noticed the missing mats. To assuage his guilt, he had saved part of his allowance every week to help pay for Sissie's doctor bills — so far he had accumulated $3.89. Sue held the three crumpled bills out to Jan.

"He felt too ashamed to give this to you himself." Tears glistened in Sue Weigle's eyes, and her voice cracked.

"Mark's a good, kind boy, Sue. You should be proud of him. He has nothing to be ashamed of. The accident wasn't his fault."

"But he's having nightmares about Sissie's accident. Guilt is eating away at him. He wants to do more than just give money if he can."

"Good. We need help. Send Mark over after school every day to take Sissie for a short walk. She needs slow, steady exercise now to strengthen those leg muscles that have become weak from inactivity."

"Mark's weak too," Sue started to cry openly now. "I think that he identifies with Sissie and wants her to be strong, just as he wishes that he could be strong."

"Sue, stop imagining things and send that boy over here after school and on Saturdays and let me put him to work as a dog therapist. He can help with massage, walking, and generally keeping up Sissie's morale during her rehabilitation. And be sure to tell Mark something: I am solely responsible for Sissie's accident. *I* forgot to replace the mats."

The next morning, Sunday, Jan and Gil took Sissie to obediance school for the first time since the accident. Trainer Jim sipped black coffee and smoked while he watched Gil gait Sissie. Stretching her legs in the spring grass, Sissie moved smoothly, though at a slow pace.

"Not too bad," was Jim's verdict. "She's a little slow, but there's scarcely any limp. And remember, folks, there's no place to go but up."

Sissie was happy to be back at obedience school after having spent so much time at home. Her tail fanned the air at old friends like Whiskey, the golden retriever, and Devil, the black Labrador; even Trainer Jim earned a tail wag and a lick on the fingers. Only Sally, the Saint Bernard, remained a menace to be avoided.

Sissie's leg still felt a little stiff, and her heeling was only fair that day, but once she was moving she felt good. When Gil got out the dumbbell, Sissie pranced around in a frenzy of excitement. Even after such a long break in training, her retrieving was excellent, though she sat slowly when she returned to heel.

"Don't worry about slow sits," Jim reassured Gil. "Very few judges will penalize you much for that. As long as Sissie is able to jump, she'll get a good score. But jumping will be the real test of her recovery. And we'll start right now."

"Now?" Gil gasped. "Isn't that too soon?"

"No. We'll set the jump at six inches today, and every lesson we'll increase the height by two inches until we're up to twenty-four inches. If she progresses OK, you can plan on trying for that last leg of her CDX by late summer or early fall."

The six-inch-high hurdle looked strange to Sissie. It was like starting kindergarten again. Just a little hop, really, and she cleared the jump. Over and back, over and back, Gil led her. Then he threw the dumbbell over the miniature hurdle and sent her for it. Sissie hopped over, seized the dumbbell, hopped back, and presented it to Gil. It was so easy that she wondered why Gil praised her so lavishly. Sissie wagged all over with happiness as Gil made a big fuss over her. Not only was her leg feeling much better, but Gil was pleased with her again.

Sissie's rehabilitation was a group effort. Everyday after school, Mark Weigle hurried over to High Point to take Sissie for a stroll. A slow pace suited the pair. Every evening after supper, when the air was cooler, Gil walked Sissie about one-half mile at first, then, as emerald May turned to moss-green June and then to parched, golden July, for longer and longer distances. In the cool mornings, it was Jan's turn to attach Sissie's leash and hit the road. Lotus went along on these morning excursions. They didn't jog, just walked at an even pace. After two months, Sissie was much less tired when they returned home.

In addition to the exercise program Jan twice daily massaged the injured leg with liniment, which kept Sissie's sable red coat a sticky mess, but Sissie liked the warmth of the ointment and stretched out her leg gratefully while Jan rubbed.

More and more, Sissie felt like running and playing with Rocky, who, at six months, was nearly full grown. But mostly Sissie lazed on the patio and just watched Rocky whirl around the fenced grounds of High Point until even the leggy puppy tired and flopped to rest panting beside her.

Gradually, the active new pattern of Sissie's days made her eyes sparkle again and brought back her appetite. By the Fourth of July, Sissie was clearing a twenty-inch hurdle with no sign of pain or effort. The Daltons were jubilant. Sissie was getting well.

19

The Test

It remained to be proven whether Sissie could jump the required heights and distances under the stressful conditions of a dog show, however. Sooner or later Gil and Jan would learn the truth. Had Sissie made a full recovery? Or was she an impaired dog who would have to be retired from obedience competition?

"Even if Sissie's show days are over," Jan tried to console Gil, "she may be a wonderful mother, and of course she'll always be our dear friend."

"But we came so close, Jan. Sissie needs only one more qualifying score to earn her CDX. I've already got the spot picked out where I want to hang her certificate."

In mid-July the Daltons decided to take a short vacation to Door County Peninsula in northern Wisconsin, just meandering and browsing as the spirit moved them. The dogs were to be boarded at a kennel owned by old friends of the Daltons, the Schroeders, who raised dachshunds.

On the way to the kennel, Lotus and Sissie slumped on the back seat of the station wagon, miserable that the calm pattern of their days was being disrupted. The suitcases had tipped them off. Rocky, who had never been boarded and so didn't suspect what was in store for him, constantly teased Sissie and tried to nip her paws.

After a pat and "Be good dogs" from Jan and Gil, the dogs were taken to separate kennel runs. Ears back, tail between her legs, Sissie dejectedly followed Roger the kennel attendant to a steel cage, the back of which opened to an outdoor run. The heavy odor of antiseptic sickened Sissie, and the smoke from Roger's cigarette stung her eyes and made them water. Roger patted Sissie's head, locked the cage, and left her alone.

Sissie felt deserted. Gil and Jan had left her in this terrible place. As far as Sissie knew, Lotus and Rocky also had deserted her. She spent the afternoon crouched miserably in her hot cage. Only after sundown did she feel like exploring her run, which was fenced off from others like it by a steel mesh fence five feet high. When Roger came to feed her and give her fresh water, cigarette smoke once again irritated her eyes and nose. She was too hot and dejected to eat.

Darkness, at least, brought relief from the heat. As the sun set, the outside runs came alive with dachshunds, some rusty brown, some black and tan, but all barking shrilly and leaping up on their short legs to see Sissie, the stranger. Sissie felt nervous at first, but, glad of some company, soon accepted her lively neighbors.

Sissie thought that she heard Rocky's bark above the shrill yapping of the dachshunds, but she couldn't see him. As she impatiently pawed the fence trying to get out, Sissie discovered that by hooking her nails through the mesh fence she could stand on her hind legs and hold herself erect. This gave her a better view, even if she was still a prisoner.

Later Roger locked the dogs in their cages for the night. When he patted Sissie's head, she wagged her tail feebly, happy for a little attention in this dreary place. Then there was nothing to do but curl up and try to sleep.

The next two days passed in deadly monotony. The heat wave continued. Sissie's cage was hot, but her unshaded run was hotter. Frequently cooling her parched tongue and dry throat with the fresh water that Roger brought, she crouched in her cage as still as possible.

Sissie liked Roger. She even licked his fingers in spite of the hated tobacco taste. Once he flicked his cigarette into the brush-covered lot behind the kennel runs, and smoke from dying embers made Sissie's eyes water. But Roger was her only family now that Gil and Jan had disappeared.

On Sunday Sissie again smelled smoke, but the odor was stronger than from the wisps of cigarette smoke. The restless dachshunds yipped at every grasshopper that bounced into the kennel runs. Sissie drank some water, then curled up with her nose tucked under her tail to shut out the acrid odor. But the noisy dachshunds and the burning smell kept her awake.

A sudden crackling sound sent Sissie outside to investigate. Grayish-black clouds swirled across the field behind the kennel, while orange flames crept menacingly toward the kennel runs.

At first, Sissie and the dachshunds leaped wildly against the fence in a frenzy to escape. Sissie barked for Roger, but no one came. Blinking to protect her eyes from the stinging smoke, she jumped again at the fence. This time her nails hooked through the wire mesh, enabling her to gain a foothold. Carefully she drew each paw upward. Sissie was climbing the fence!

But she faced the serious problem of how to hoist her eighteen pounds over the top of the fence. With her front paws as close to the top as possible, she drew up her hind legs as high as she could without losing her balance, then hurtled headfirst over the fence and leaped to the ground.

As Sissie ran for help past the long row of kennel runs, a familiar scent stopped her. She followed the scent around the corner to a similar row of runs until, with a yelp of recognition, she leaped against Lotus's run.

Wagging her tail, Lotus ran eagerly to greet Sissie. All past differences forgotten, they wiggled together nose to nose.

"Sissie! How did you get out?" Roger exclaimed, appearing suddenly from the kennel office holding a blaring transistor radio. He slipped a choke collar around Sissie's neck and jerked her angrily.

"What ails those silly weiner dogs? And you, you bad dog, could get me fired if you ran away. I thought you were my friend, Sissie. Bad dog! Hey, what's that funny smell?"

With a last look toward Lotus and a pleading glance at Roger, Sissie forged ahead to make Roger hurry.

When Roger saw the smoke, he dropped Sissie's leash and ran toward the fire. Quickly, he unlocked the runs, releasing the dachshunds. Only a few yards away the fire raged in spurts to swallow a thicket of weeds, then slowly crept toward the next meal of dry twigs.

With a towel over his head for protection against smoke and heat, Roger ran to the office and called the fire department. Meanwhile, the dachshunds scattered in panic at the fire and bewilderment over their sudden freedom.

Then Sissie took charge. Barking, she dove for the largest male dachshund, snapping at the glossy black flanks of the terrified dog. In the face of this new threat, he stopped running. A young female raced by him. Sissie headed her off with a series of staccato barks. The fear-driven dachshunds stopped running as Sissie herded them

like sheep. The sable Sheltie's fury combined with their terror kept them huddled together for safety.

When Roger finally came running out of the office with a tangle of leashes, the weary dachshunds let themselves be leashed and led to shelter. All fourteen were safe.

Panting heavily, bone-weary from her ordeal, Sissie followed Roger into the kennel office and lay down to rest beside Lotus, Rocky, and the fourteen dachshunds. The three Shelties had a happy reunion, nuzzling each other affectionately.

That night, long after the fire had been extinguished, a cool breeze ended the hot spell. Lotus, Sissie, and Rocky stretched out to sleep side by side.

When Jan and Gil, tanned and rested from their vacation, came for the dogs Monday morning, the story of Sissie's heroism was told and retold. The Schroeders refused to take any money for boarding the three Shelties.

"Sissie earned her keep," Bob Schroeder said, patting Sissie's red sable head. "It's a miracle that none of the dogs was hurt. Ann and I were at a dog show all day Sunday. I suspect the fire started from a discarded cigarette, and I made my kennel boy promise to give up smoking on the job."

Bob Schroeder and Gil shook hands. Then Sissie, Lotus, and Rocky jumped into the station wagon to go home. How wonderful to get home again, to race across the tree-shaded lawn and sprawl lazily on the shady end of the patio.

"Do you know what I'm *really* thrilled about?" Jan asked as she sorted laundry from the trip.

"What?"

"Sissie's passed a really important test."

"What kind of test?"

"Why, she climbed! That required complete control of her hind legs and the strength to support her weight as she climbed and then jumped down. And she still had enough stamina to herd those cute little dachshunds."

"You're right. I was so relieved that the dogs were safe, I didn't analyze the situation. By the way, are you sure that Sissie actually climbed? Did anyone see her?"

"No, but Roger is certain of it. He says that the runs and cages were locked securely and, unless Sissie sprouted wings, she had to climb to escape."

Gently, Gil held Sissie's head between his hands.

"Sissie, you're well. I think we can be certain of it."

20

The Cow Jumped Over the Moon

So excited were the Daltons about Sissie's progress that they sent in entries for two dog shows in hope that Sissie could qualify for the one leg needed to finish her CDX title.

"We'll have to work hard," Gil admitted, "to make up for all the lost training time. But Jim thinks that we can do it."

Sissie was so happy to be working regularly again with Gil that she leaped high into the air and nipped playfully at Gil's arm when he took her collar, leash, and dumbbell out of the closet. During lessons, she paid attention and worked well, sailing over the high jump as though the tendon in her leg had never been injured.

But the broad jump was another story. This hurdle, which consisted of three very low boards spaced out to a distance of four feet, gave Sissie trouble. Before the accident, she had jumped the hurdle effortlessly, but now Sissie was not sure how much thrust would carry her over the jump or how much of a running start she needed. Over and over Gil jumped with her to try to build up her confidence but left to perform the exercise on her own, Sissie hopped across each board separately instead of altogether. The few times that she tried to jump all the boards at once, she landed short and bruised her paws on the last board. That made her stop trying.

"Sissie, what's the matter with you?" Gil yelled the first time that Sissie walked across the boards instead of jumping.

"Jan, look what Sissie's doing! Walking the broad jump! That's an automatic disqualification in a show."

"Take it easy," warned Jan. "Sissie's lost her timing, just like any athlete after an injury. She'll get it back. Give her time."

Then Gil tried placing another board diagonally on top of the broad jump to make it appear higher. That time Sissie cleared the hurdle with room to spare. When he removed the extra board, she once again stepped over each board separately.

"It looks too flat to her," Jan concluded. "She can't gauge how high to jump. Besides, her leg may be stiffening up. We must be careful not to overwork that leg."

"But the show's next weekend," Gil despaired.

"Then let's not go if you're worried."

"Not go? But we've paid our ten dollars entry fee, and Sissie might just surprise us. Let's give it a try. Like Jim said, there's no place to go but up."

"Sissie waved her white-tipped plume of a tail happily. Her favorite people were talking about her, petting her, and giving her all their attention. And that was heaven to Sissie.

Jan and Gil could only guess, of course, how Sissie felt. They watched closely for signs of pain or strain when Sissie ran or jumped. They saw none. Only, when Sissie got up and stretched after sprawling on the den rug, did she look a bit stiff? Of did Jan and Gil only imagine it? But Sissie had resumed playing rough-and-tumble games with Rocky with no hint of pain shadowing her dark, almond-shaped eyes.

In spite of Gil's doubts, they went to the show that Saturday. It was a typical summer dog show: a huge red and white candy-striped canopy billowed in the middle of a sometime soccer field jammed with cars, campers, grooming tables, wire crates, exercise pens, people, and — in all shapes, sizes, colors, and with barks pitched from basso to falsetto — dogs.

Underlying the flood of sights and sounds was a medley of smells peculiar to dog shows: hairspray, coat dressing, chalk dust,

hot coffee, and that pungent odor that preceded a blaring call over the loudspeaker for a clean-up boy.

At first, Sissie felt uncomfortable in this noisy, bustling scene, but after Gil gave her a piece of glazed donut, she felt much better. And when Gil got the dumbbell out of his pocket, Sissie knew that she was here to have some fun.

At promptly eleven o'clock, Sissie's obedience class, Open A, began. The sun was hot, but dark clouds glowered from the northwest. A canopy-style tent shaded spectators and dogs awaiting their turn in the ring, but the obedience rings themselves were not sheltered.

"Where do we take cover if it rains?" Jan asked. "Under the tent?"

"No way," Gil warned. "That flimsy canopy will fold in a high wind. Best bet is to run for the car."

As the winds heightened, the canopy alternately ballooned with gusts, then sagged heavily. Gil nervously started to warm up Sissie with some fast heeling under the tent. Sissie hated the crowded place. Everywhere she looked loomed a behemoth of a Saint Bernard or Great Pyrenees, Russian wolfhound, Great Dane or briard. An occasional terrier or cocker spaniel met her at eye level, but mostly big dogs, not all friendly, stared at Sissie and made concentration on work difficult.

Only two dogs remained before Sissie's turn in the ring. So far, very few dogs had passed all the exercises.

"The dogs sense the storm," was Jan's theory.

Now only one dog remained before Sissie. The black miniature poodle heeled at a fast clip beside his quick-paced young handler. But just as the boy threw the dumbbell, a lightning bolt spiked the sky, followed by a thunderclap that sent the poodle dashing out of the ring in terror. The boy ran after Jock, the poodle, but the dog panicked and eluded his master and everyone else who tried to catch him.

As though some celestial, water-filled balloon had been pricked by that lightning bolt, rain lashed by high winds now deluged the dog show grounds.

"Run for the car!" Gil yelled, picking up Sissie to keep her from being trampled by the stampeding herd of people and dogs who rushed out from under the tent.

"Evacuate the tents, evacuate the tents," warned the loudspeaker. "Ladies and gentlemen, please seek cover with your dogs. Do not panic. Your cars will keep you safe. Rubber tires protect against lightning. Do not panic, but seek cover promptly. Please *do not,* I repeat *do not* remain under the tents."

Hunched against what felt like a wall of water, Jan and Gil struggled to their station wagon. They were almost there when they heard the boy crying for his poodle.

"Jock, Jock, where are you? Come here, Jock. Don't get lost and hurt, Jock, please don't be hurt." Then the boy's parents pulled him into the green station wagon parked five or six cars down from the Daltons.

Gil opened the car door for Jan, who sagged in like wet laundry, dripping all over the upholstery.

"Here, take Sissie, I'm going back to look for Jock."

But Sissie squirmed out of Jan's arms and ran after Gil through the mud of the rutted dirt road back to the now-disheveled rings covered by a billowing canopy that strained like a zeppelin at its moorings and alternately threatened to collapse and to blow away.

Gil remembered seeing Jock scoot under the judge's table in one of the rings and hide behind a red and white picnic hamper. If the tent collapsed on the dog, he could be smothered or crushed easily.

Nothing looked the same as before. The wind had rearranged the equipment, toppling ring standards, obedience jumps, and judges' tables. Sissie barked excitedly as she followed Gil, who had difficulty seeing through a curtain of rain.

Sissie heard the whining coming from behind the red and white picnic hamper wedged under a table that had toppled onto its side to

form a lean-to. Against this makeshift shelter, Jock had taken refuge from the storm. Drenched, the black poodle huddled against the turned-over table.

When Gil reached for Jock, the poodle growled menacingly.

"Uh, oh, Sissie, we've got a problem." As Gil spoke, the wind seemed to intensify its fury.

Sissie sniffed cautiously at the picnic hamper. Gil opened it and dumped out its contents of ham sandwiches and cookies. He took some ham out of a sandwich and offered some to Jock and some to Sissie. Sissie grabbed hers, delighted to receive such a delicacy under any conditions. Jock wasn't too interested, but while he was thinking about whether to eat the ham, Gil popped the empty hamper over him and deftly scooped him into it, flipping the lid closed.

Once more Gil and Sissie made the tortuous trip against the wind back to the car, where a worried Jan had towels and a car blanket waiting. Gil's arms ached from carrying the struggling Jock in the hamper.

Jock's reunion with his family was a very happy one, with even some chuckles over the trapping of the poodle in the hamper. Gil brought the empty hamper back to the car with him. By now the rain had stopped.

"Ladies and gentlemen," boomed the loudspeaker to a much-diminished crowd, "judging will resume as soon as we can reconstruct the rings. Please prepare your dogs for judging."

"Are they kidding? Make dogs jump on wet grass?" Gil was shocked at the idea.

"But we've suffered through this mess so far, why not chance it?"

"No way, Jan. Sissie could reinjure her leg if she slipped on wet grass. If the motor in this Chevy still works after all that rain, we're going to get out of here."

The car started and inched forward through mud and wet gravel to the highway. The Daltons and Sissie headed home for baths and warm food.

* * * *

When they were dry and comfortable again and Sissie was tumbling with Rocky on the den rug, Gil remembered something.

"Good Lord, Jan, I've got some judge's picnic hamper and I ruined his lunch."

Jan laughed hysterically while Sissie jumped up and licked her face, wanting to share the fun.

"Maybe he'll think the wind blew it away," Jan said, her face contorted with laughter.

"Remember that nursery rhyme, Gil?"

"Hey diddle diddle
The cat and the fiddle,
The cow jumped over the moon;
The little dog laughed
To see such sport
And the dish ran away with the spoon.

"Well, that reminds me of what happened today. It was a crazy, nonsense world out there today. Nothing made sense. Maybe the dogs were laughing."

"And maybe the judge will think that his dishes and spoons and hamper ran away with his ham sandwiches and chocolate chip cookies."

Jan wiped tears of laughter from her eyes and blew her nose.

"One thing bothers me, though," she snorted through a tissue.

"What's that?"

"The cow jumped over the moon. But will Sissie jump over the broad jump? We still don't know."

"No, we still don't know, do we, Sissie?" said Gil, rumpling Sissie's ears while the sable and white Sheltie thumped her tail happily against his leg.

21

An Interpretation of Rules

The following day, Sunday, the weather promised to behave. The only trace of yesterday's deluge was an extra helping of glittering dew on the lush grass.

"Do you think that the grass will be too wet for Sissie to jump safely?" Jan worried out loud. "We could stay home and wait for indoor shows this winter."

"From the looks of that clear sky and bright sun," said Gil, getting Sissie's collar and leash out of the hall closet, "I'd say that by ten o'clock the grass will be dry. Let's go, Sissie."

With Sissie sprawled on the back seat, happy to be going, the miseries of the previous day forgotten, they drove south for an hour down the coast of Lake Michigan to a park that laced the rocky shore like a green shoestring.

The scene at the show was very much a repeat of the day before except that the air was calm and crisp, cleared of turbulence, and people and dogs had more room to spread out. Hot coffee and Danish rolls perked up the Daltons after the long ride. Sissie shared a cinnamon pastry with Jan.

"Looks like we've got some competition," Gil pointed in the catalogue to the name of one of the best obedience Shelties in the Midwest — Copperwood Teacup Tempest, or "Tempo," as he was called by his owner, Linda Sutton, a well-known dog trainer. Just as Gil predicted, Tempo turned in the polished performance expected from a veteran obedience dog and frequent High in Trial winner. Since Tempo already had his CDX, he was entered in Open B, a special class for such advanced dogs.

"The dog works like a machine," Jan whispered after the applause for Tempo had died down. "No spirit, no vivacity like Sissie has when she works."

"Well, this isn't a personality contest, you know. Accuracy counts the most."

"Don't the rules state that a dog must be a willing worker?"

"True, but it's all a matter of how the judge interprets the rules and the dog's performance. The rules call for 'willingness, enjoyment, and precision' on the part of the dog and 'smoothness and gentleness' in handling. But the judge has to decide whether those standards are being met."

Gil fished the dumbbell out of his pocket and played with Sissie for a few minutes to work out any stiffness in her leg. And then it was their turn to compete in the Open A class, the class for dogs who were trying to earn their CDX titles.

"Good luck," Jan crossed her fingers and said a silent prayer.

Sissie heeled very well, shadowing Gil's left heel without crowding him. Their "figure eight" was a model of dog-handler teamwork. Then Gil left Sissie at the far end of the ring for the drop on recall exercise. He called her and, at the judge's signal, told her to "down." She dropped in her tracks, then, on command, trotted happily in to Gil, tail waving, and sat squarely in front of him.

The retrieving exercises were Sissie's favorites. Joyfully, she dashed out to get her dumbbell as though an Obedience Trial were the greated fun in the world. Gil felt tense as he took the dumbbell from Sissie. The jumping exercises came next.

Gil took his position in front of the two-foot-high jump and, at the judge's command, threw the dumbbell, but whether from nervousness or sheer clumsiness, he threw poorly, and the dumbbell struck the top of the jump, then bounced over the hurdle in two pieces.

There was a gasp from the crowd. Jan covered her face with her hands in disappointment. Sissie's performance was spoiled.

Gil had forgotten to bring his spare dumbbell. The awareness of this oversight turned his spine to ice as he listened to the judge tell him that he could repeat the exercise with a new dumbbell or send his dog to get one of the two pieces of the broken dumbbell.

Gil turned around and looked at Jan. She shrugged, not knowing what to do. Then the young owner of the poodle Jock ran up to Gil with a dumbbell.

"Here, take Jock's, he won't mind," said the boy.

Gil had only a second to decide. Should he risk throwing a strange dumbbell for Sissie, one that held another dog's scent? Or should he trust Sissie to bring back one of the pieces of her own dumbbell? He shook his head "no" at Jock's master.

"Sissie, take!" Gil thundered resolutely. The sable and white Sheltie, wondering why all the delay, took a running start and hurtled over the high jump with plenty of room to spare. But if ever an obedience dog was called on to think, this was the time. Before Sissie lay a dilemma — two objects instead of one. But Sissie knew that Gil scolded her for dawdling. She had no intention of loitering now. Without hesitation, Sissie seized the larger piece and sailed back over the hurdle, landing squarely in front of Gil with the piece of dumbbell dangling lopsidedly from her jaws and a questioning look in her eyes.

While the crowd applauded, Gil praised Sissie enormously.

The broad jump was next. Gil knew that this would be the real test of Sissie's recovery, because the accident had spoiled her timing on this exercise.

Gil and Sissie faced the broad jump from eight feet away. At the judge's command, Gil told Sissie to stay and walked to the side of the low hurdle.

"Send your dog," ordered the judge.

"Sissie, over!" called Gil, with the hint of prayer in his voice. Sissie stood up, eyed the jump as if sizing up the distance that her muscles would be required to propel her, took a few tentative steps forward, then hurtled over the four-foot broad jump. Then she turned and trotted in to sit in front of Gil. On command, Sissie swung smartly to heel, looking up to Gil for approval.

This time the applause for Sissie was even more enthusiastic, and Gil praised her as never before. She had proven that she could once again do the difficult jumping demanded at an Obedience Trial.

At ringside, Jan hugged and kissed Sissie. Sissie showed appreciation by licking away the salty tears that moistened Jan's face, while Gil blew his nose and pretended that something had blown into his eye.

So far, Sissie had turned in the best performance of her life. Only the long sit and long down exercises separated her from the coveted Companion Dog Excellent title. Twelve dogs of assorted breeds lined up to sit for three minutes and then lie down for five minutes with their handlers out of sight. This was a real test of a dog's steadiness and dependability.

The long sit was uneventful, except for a basenji that started to scratch, then lay down.

On the long down, a German shepherd started to creep toward Sissie. She held her ground and ignored the restless shepherd, even when he sniffed curiously. Sissie knew that this was not the time to make friends.

The handlers returned, and the judge uttered those wonderful words "exercise finished." Nothing remained now but to await his decision on what dogs had qualified and which of these had won prizes.

That Sissie's number — 133 — was among those called back into the ring was no surprise to the Daltons. But when the judge announced that number 133 had won first place in Open A class with 197½ points out of a possible 200, they were ecstatic. The gleaming copper trophy that Gil received was icing on the cake.

At ringside, Jan again had some news for Gil: Tempo had won first in his class, Open B, with the exact score as Sissie. So far, the two Shelties were tied for Highest Scoring Dog in the trial. But only one dog could win that honor.

"Let's eat while we're waiting," said Gil. "All this excitement has given me a terrific appetite."

They dined on hot dogs and canned cola. Sissie eagerly gobbled the bite of hot dog that Jan gave her — eating such exotic tidbits was the best part of dog shows.

By three o'clock the judging of all obedience classes had been completed, and no other dogs had scored higher than Sissie and Tempo. A runoff was called for.

So, even though they were tired after the long, demanding trial, Gil and Sissie faced Linda Sutton and Tempo in a runoff for Highest Scoring Dog in the trial. A different judge now faced them, one who had not previously judged either dog that day. The runoff exercise, the judge said, would consist of heeling off leash; the dog that made the first mistake would be eliminated instantly.

"Are you ready?" asked the judge, a tanned, athletic man wearing a wide-brimmed straw hat.

Both handlers nodded.

"Forward!" snapped the judge, and the contest was underway.

Both Shelties worked flawlessly. The crowd was hushed. Which dog would make the first mistake? Jan's hands were clenched from the tension.

As she watched, Jan noticed the difference between the way in which the two dogs worked. Sissie held her head and tail up and looked happy; Tempo, on the other hand, held his head down as though ready to dodge a blow. Not that Jan had ever seen Mrs. Sutton hit the dog. But there had been rumors — and Linda Sutton made it no secret that she took "no nonsense" from her dog.

Once more the judge ordered Gil and Mrs. Sutton to heel their dogs down the ring, barking out "slow," "fast," and "halt" commands to see how the dogs adapted to changes of pace. On the next about turn, Tempo ducked his head, making it appear that he lagged a fraction. Without hesitation the judge pointed to Sissie as the winner.

"Sheltie number 133 wins the runoff," he announced, and the crowd roared its approval. Sissie had become a favorite after her

Jan had to help Gil carry the impressive silver tea service awarded to Sissie in addition to a check for $100. Everyone congratulated the Daltons and praised Sissie. Everyone, that is, except Mrs. Sutton.

"According to the rules," she was heard telling the judge, Bob Nelson, "my dog did not lag. He did not make a mistake."

"According to the rules, Madam," Nelson retorted, "I may penalize a handler for militarylike precision in handling his dog. I felt that your motions were robotlike, not natural, and that the dog responded without natural eagerness. The other Sheltie worked eagerly and happily. That's my interpretation of the rules, and I'd like to see you challenge me before the American Kennel Club."

Mrs. Sutton sputtered but kept silent, realizing that an outburst could jeopardize her showing future. She turned and left the ring.

Bob Nelson congratulated the Daltons, then took off his straw hat and reached for a glass of water. It was hot, but the Daltons had been too busy to notice.

"What a weekend, folks,' Nelson sighed. "Yesterday I judged at that terrible rain-out of a show, and some thief stole my lunch hamper and tore my sandwiches apart in the bargain — snitched the ham right out from between the bread. So I had to settle for the usual hot dogs, which irritated my ulcer. And today I may just succumb from heat stroke."

He paused to drink, then stooped down and patted Sissie.

"But I did see one fine-working Sheltie," he said. "It was a pleasure to judge such an eager worker. Best of luck to you in future shows."

As Gil shook hands with Bob Nelson, he wondered whether to return the red and white hamper, which he still had in his car. But how could he explain his possession of the judge's property without looking like a fool, or, worse, like a thief?

Jan wrapped the silver tea set carefully in the car blanket to protect it on the way home. Then Gil placed Bob Nelson's picnic hamper on the grass at the edge of the show grounds.

"Hopefully, someone will turn it in to the superintendent's office. I'll be darned if I'm going to try to explain how I ruined the digestion of a judge that just awarded me and Sissie Highest Scoring Dog in Trial."

Jan laughed sympathetically.

"What a wonderful dog show, what a perfect day," she said. "Sissie wins her CDX title and a High in Trial and defeats one of the top dogs in the country. Sissie, you're beautiful."

As for Sissie — no matter that Gil had asked her to retrieve the weirdest-looking dumbbell she had ever seen — any day that Jan and Gil made a fuss over her and fed her Danish pastry and hot dogs was a beautiful day indeed.

22

The Old Order Changeth

When Sissie's CDX certificate arrived, it was beautifully framed and hung in the den to be admired. Sissie's training was by no means ended; Gil began teaching her even more advanced exercises such as the bar jump and scent discrimination, of which she already knew the basics. But Sissie was a mature Sheltie now, and the Daltons had an important decision to make about her future.

The time came early in September when Sissie could be bred if a suitable mate were found for her. The Daltons had given this matter of a proper mate for Sissie considerable thought and had selected Crestline Kennels, a small kennel but one noted for sound, fine-quality Shetland sheepdogs.

Sissie enjoyed the ride. Her ears tipped forward alertly as the car approached the driveway that led to the kennel. With her inquisitive nose far out of the car window, Sissie caught the scent of strange dogs.

The kennel grounds were beautiful: blue spruce, pine, a grove of red maples, beds of crimson canna lilies, and purple-tinged asters delighted the senses with color and fragrance. When the kennel dogs heard the visitors' car, the warning bark carried from dog to dog until a multipitched chorus of barks and yelps provided background music for the panorama of autumn color.

"So this is the famous Sissie," said Mrs. Sechrist, a lanky, middle-aged woman with short-cropped graying hair who, dressed in green tweed slacks and a green turtleneck sweater, seemed youthful and vigorous.

"She certainly is a lovely Sheltie," said Mrs. Sechrist, extending her hand for Sissie to sniff. "And smart too, I hear."

At mention of her name and encouraged by Mrs. Sechrist's friendly voice, Sissie sniffed the hand that smelled faintly of liver and dogs.

"I think that she likes me," said the kindly woman. "I can see that Sissie's not shy. That's good."

Then Mrs. Sechrist examined Sissie to see what her best points were and if she had any faults that would have to be compensated for in a mate. A dog with too-fine bone, for instance, would be mated with a heavier-boned dog so that the puppies would be sound.

Mrs. Sechrist found Sissie sound, strong, and in excellent health.

"Let's look around a bit," she suggested, and Sissie trotted willingly along to the source of all the intriguing scents and sounds that had tantalized her from the driveway.

The Crestline Shelties lived royally in outside kennels, each with a large doghouse on a raised platform. Living outdoors all year was good for the Shelties' coats. The Crestline dogs seemed happy, healthy, and friendly, leaping playfully against the fences of their kennel runs when Sissie approached.

Sissie was overjoyed to have found so many potential playmates. But the dog that really caught her attention did not seem to be friendly at all. Dignified and aloof, he stood back and surveyed the visitors.

Sissie gazed fascinated at the exquisite Sheltie, Champion Crestline King's Coronet. Like an arrogant lord looking down at his subjects, he stood at the entrance to his raised shelter, only slightly interested in Sissie.

King was breathtakingly handsome and represented years of careful breeding. A little larger than Sissie, he carried an extraordinary heavy red sable coat that made him look as though he had just come from a winter climate. A wide, white ruff framed his throat like the collars of stiff white lace worn by Elizabethan lords. Although well marked with white on his chest and forelegs, he had no white on his face, which gave him a serious, intent expression. His dark, almond-shaped eyes showed intelligence. At four years old, King stood in the prime of life, already the sire of several Champions. Sissie looked through the fence, wagging her tail and inviting King to play.

For awhile after he saw Sissie, King remained aloof. However, when the russet Sheltie with the warm, gentle brown eyes wagged her plumed tail, he paraded majestically down the ramp for a closer look. Sissie nuzzled the fence.

King wagged his tail sedately in greeting. Then down went his forequarters, up went his rump in the ridiculous puppy attitude of play. While Mrs. Sechrist opened the gate, Gil unfastened Sissie's leash and let her run inside. King, tail playfully waving, chest puffing marshmallow white, pranced to meet her, whining joyfully at this beautiful new friend.

* * * *

After the visit to Crestline Kennels, life for Sissie lost much of its savor. Everything seemed different. Even playing with the old knotted sock that Gil tossed for her on crisp autumn mornings seemed monotonous. Food interested her even less. More and more, she sulked under the bed and growled at Lotus and Rocky. Lotus tried to squelch the mutiny by lowering her head and baring her fangs, but this had no effect on the moody Sissie.

The Daltons were concerned with the growing feud between the two dogs. It was a long time since they had considered getting rid of one of their pets; even when they had thought seriously about it, they had been unable to choose. But with Sissie expecting puppies, they felt that a decision could not be postponed much longer.

Jan and Gil discussed the problem in the den one evening while they were having their usual snack of coffee and cookies.

"It might be a good idea if we boarded Lotus until Sissie has her puppies," Jan suggested. "We certainly can't have the dogs constantly growling and snarling at each other."

"Let's wait and see," Gil cautioned. "That would be a drastic change for Lotus at her age."

"Well, let's board Sissie, then. She's younger and could make the adjustment more easily. We could pay for her board with a puppy."

Gil liked that idea even less. They let the matter rest.

October was damp and cold, and as the dogs spent more time indoors, their tempers grew raw. Sometimes Sissie gnawed brazenly on Lotus's leather "bone," and when Lotus would try to reclaim her toy, Sissie's sweet Sheltie smile would become a snarl. A sharp reprimand by Jan erased the snarl, but left Sissie sullen. Fretful and peevish, she tried everyone's patience.

"That settles it!" Gil declared one day when he found Lotus and Sissie slavering at each other like predatory wolves over which Sheltie would enter the den first. "I'm going to call Mrs. Sechrist to ask if she'll take Sissie for a month or so. Maybe Sissie's manners will improve."

Jan frowned but went along with the idea.

Three evenings after he had taken Sissie to Crestline, Gil received a call from Mrs. Sechrist asking him to come for Sissie. Sissie refused to eat and seemed terribly homesick. Mrs. Sechrist was afraid that Sissie would become ill if she continued to sulk. Even King had not been able to cheer up the brooding Sissie.

Sissie was happy to be home. The next morning, however, when Jan called her into the kitchen for a special breakfast of cereal and milk, Lotus leaped without warning at Sissie's throat, knocking her down and threatening the younger dog until Sissie froze belly-up in the wild's gesture of surrender. Jan knew that Lotus did not really want to hurt Sissie, only to establish her own authority. Lotus couldn't understand why the younger dog now deserved special treats and attention.

Lotus stepped back snarling. Sissie got up and waited, hackles bristling, facing Lotus not as a daughter but as an equal. If war was to be declared, she would fight. Gradually, the snarl of both dogs subsided. The battle was over.

The result of this incident was that Lotus was boarded. Perplexed, Sissie ran about the house sniffing corners, peering under beds, exploring closets, and returning frequently to the den to see if Lotus were in her accustomed place beneath the old mahogany desk.

"She'll settle down," Jan remarked at Sissie's disturbing behavior.

Gil agreed that some restless behavior on Sissie's part was natural. But Sissie continued to search for Lotus. Most often, however, she crawled under the den desk and curled up there, gazing mournfully at Jan, who tried to coax her out. She refused to play with Rocky. And even the old knotted sock lost its charm for Sissie.

As October ended and frost hardened the earth, Sissie spent more and more of her time sleeping, always under the old mahogany desk now, quiet and very lonely. For the truth was that Sissie missed her mother a great deal. All the growling and baring of fangs had meant little compared to the deep and enduring affection that Sissie felt for Lotus. The two dogs had never hurt one another, although the gestures of fierceness had alarmed Jan and Gil. Now, with both her people away working all day, the puppy Rocky annoyed Sissie and her days were empty.

It hurt Jan and Gil to see Sissie so listless, wandering the house searching for her mother like a lost orphan. They admitted that they had made a mistake.

One Saturday morning, Gil went out early and returned with Lotus, who raced around the grounds joyfully, home again where she belonged.

Jan let Sissie out the back door. For a moment, the two Shelties stared at each other, trying to understand the strange disappearances that plagued and confused them in the world of humans. With a volley of high-pitched yelps, Sissie flung herself like a bronze whirlwind, heavy though she was with her coming litter, against the ebony and white Sheltie who was her mother and her dearest enemy. Lotus licked Sissie's slender muzzle and soft ears as if Sissie were her little puppy again. Then the two nipped each other in mock attack, growling as fiercely as they could through their joy.

Very early the next morning, Sissie became a mother.

Lotus, finally allowed into the kitchen, found Gil and Jan looking down on a very tired Sissie who had been joined in the whelping box by four tiny, wriggling, sable and white puppies.

"They're beautiful," Jan exclaimed, tired after a night of sitting up with Sissie. "They'll all be Champions."

Gil agreed. "And obedience champions as well," he added.

Sissie's eyes radiated concern as she surveyed her new little family and busily licked the helpless babies that knew no world but their mother's warm side.

Lotus approached the whelping box hesitantly, then wagged her tail at Sissie in the old invitation to play. Sissie whined low in response, too busy now for play. She had more important things to do. The tiny, ratlike puppies squealing and wriggling at her side reminded her of her new duties, and diligently, while Lotus watched from a respectful distance, Sissie continued caring for her puppies, her soft, brown eyes, as she gazed at them, full of pride, gentleness, and love.

About the Author

The subject of Shetland Sheepdogs, dog shows, and training is not new to author Joan R. Simons. A former English instructor, Ms. Simons has had articles published in *Dog World* and *The Sheltie Special,* as well as poems and articles in the *Wisconsin English Journal.*

She has shown several dogs to their Companion Dog (C.D.) and Companion Dog Excellent (C.D.X.) titles, and one to its conformation Championship. She is an active member of both the Greater Milwaukee

Shetland Sheepdog Club and the K-9 Obedience Training Club of Menomonee Falls, Wisconsin.

Joan and her husband, Sid, currently reside in Wauwatosa, Wisconsin, where she divides her time between their card and gift shop and her hobbies of writing and dog training.

Cover design: Charlotte Wolf
Book design and cover photo: Betty McKinney
Typesetting: The Type Exchange
Printing and binding: North Central Publishing Co.